HAPPILY
EVER
AFTER?

Contents

1

Happiness in Marriage: Myth or Reality?

Do you remember Cinderella, Snow White, and the miller's daughter? (Rumpelstiltskin helped her, I think.) There was also another — Rapunzel, the one with the hair.

These maidens had three things in common: They were all beautiful, they all married far above their own social and economic levels, and they all lived "happily ever after."

You, like others of us, probably grew up hearing the phrase "happily ever after" at the end of your bedtime stories. Although you knew these were just fairy tales, still you dreamed of the day when your own Prince Charming would come and sweep you off into the land of eternal wedded bliss. Right?

Later, your Young Women's teacher taught you about temple and eternal marriage. Though it might never have been said in so many words, you may have started to believe in what I call the "Mormon Myth" — if you keep yourself worthy and are married in the temple happiness is assured.

Possibly, as a consequence of this kind of wishful thinking, you have continued to ascribe a magical quality to marriage. Some may consider it to be a panacea or the secret of happiness.

But those are high, perhaps even totally unrealistic, expectations.

If a girl goes into marriage expecting that she and her husband will automatically become a celestial couple, it is little wonder that soon after the excitement of the wedding, the reception, the gifts, and the honeymoon wears off, she begins to feel uneasy. With unrealistic expectations, a young wife can't help but experience disappointment which can grow into anger, resentment, or worse, a feeling of failure with its accompanying sense of guilt. And when you are anticipating complete happiness, even the normal vicissitudes of life seem unbearable.

One bride told me that shortly after the big day she started to feel despondent, almost depressed. She also felt guilty: "Why am I feeling like this? I have a wonderful husband. I'm supposed to be the happiest girl in the world."

Another said that after several weeks of marriage she felt all of her self-confidence melt away. She didn't feel like going to work, shopping, or anywhere else. She didn't even feel like putting on her makeup.

Another bride said she cried over "the stupidest little things." If her new husband put extra salt on his dinner, she was sure he didn't like her cooking. Or, if he chose to wear a different tie than the one she set out for him, it meant he didn't like her taste.

These cases are not unusual.

Is it any wonder that this happens? After all, by all outward appearances, *other* young couples look as if they have everything under control and are living happily, just as expected.

The bride, especially, starts to question, "What is wrong with us?"

The answer, I think, is that there is nothing wrong with you, but there is a lot wrong with the idea that marriage automatically brings forth joy and happiness.

We can rid our consciences of the burden of the perfect marriage syndrome, that collection of idealistic qualities which no one can achieve quickly.

A gold wedding ring and an "I do" do not instantly change you into an ideal wife who can love and comfort her husband, overcome immediately a lifetime's conditioning regarding the avoidance of sex, keep a spotlessly clean house, serve three nutritionally balanced, attractive, economical meals each day, bake whole wheat bread, read scriptures, keep up the laundry and ironing, compile her genealogy, maintain a garden, preserve all the produce, paint the fence, balance the budget, have babies, serve in the Church and community, and . . . help!

It is no wonder brides feel overwhelmed. I am aware of the scripture, "Be ye therefore perfect, even as your Father which is in heaven is perfect" (Matthew 5:48).

But, I am also aware of this one: "To every thing there is a season, and a time to every purpose under the heaven" (Ecclesiastes 3:1). The following ten verses in Ecclesiastes specify a sample of things for which there is a time. Everything does not have to take place at the same time.

And finally, consider a verse from modern scripture: "Ye are not able to abide the presence of God now, neither the ministering of angels; wherefore, continue in patience until ye are perfected" (D&C 67:13).

Note that last phrase, "continue in patience until ye are perfected."

I love perfection and ideals. But I do not like the way we often get hampered by thinking that we are failures because we are not perfect right now. Perfection requires growth and progress, and growth and progress require time.

It's a little like telling a rambunctious seven-year-old boy that he is a failure because he isn't a stake president.

But love him, teach him, train him, and give him perhaps thirty or forty years, and he may indeed be a stake president.

So, don't panic as you wonder, "Can my husband and I be happy? Is there any hope for us?"

The answer? Yes, definitely. You can be happy—but only with much effort.

For a moment let's take a less idealistic look at marriage. About a month after the great event, you awake one morning to see your sleeping husband, a snorting, bristly man with disheveled hair, and suddenly realize you are still in the same world as the one you thought you had left behind with the dolls and teen magazines.

How appalling! I agree.

But appalling or not, it is true. While you have changed your status from single to married, just about everything else has remained the same.

Food still has to be cooked, dishes have to be done, clothes need washing, and you will feel tired, and even angry, from time to time. So will your husband.

I'm sorry, but that is how it is.

Well, now that the myth of automatic happiness in marriage is broken, you have two choices:

1. *Quit.* Statistics indicate that in 1978 there were 186,787 marriages and 55,370 divorces in Canada; in the United States there were 2,243,000 marriages and 1,128,000 divorces. (*The World Almanac and Book of Facts — 1980,* New York, Newspaper Enterprise Association.)

2. *Adjust.* Make the best of it. You are undoubtedly familiar with the phrase *adjustment to marriage.* Have you any idea what it means?

In part, marriage means adjusting, or harmonizing, your hopes, personality, habits, and daily routines to accommodate your husband's hopes, personality, habits, and daily routines.

Or, looking at it from another angle, it means that, in addition to having this great fellow with you day and night — all night every night — with his curly hair and broad shoulders, you also have him with his annoying morning lethargy, his dirty shirts, and his maddening habit of reading novels in the only bathroom.

Is it beginning to sound complicated?

President Kimball said, "Marriage is not easy; it is not simple." (Spencer W. Kimball, *Marriage and Divorce,* Deseret Book Co., 1976, page 11.)

President John K. Edmunds, former president of the Salt Lake Temple, told BYU students preparing for marriage: "We can give you the ordinance, but we can't give you eternal marriage. That is your decision; that is your job. That you must earn. You have nothing made by simply coming here. Nothing is ever made that you do not make yourself. You will have to continue in righteousness, to the end of your lives, living 'by every word that proceedeth forth from the mouth of God.' " ("1,113 Couples, But How Many Marriages?" *Ensign,* July 1976, page 69.)

Sobering, isn't it? No guarantees of happiness there. Instead, he puts the responsibility for seeking and building happiness squarely on the shoulders of each couple.

Without doubt you have taken on a big challenge.

I'm convinced that most marriages that fail do so because couples do not know how to make them succeed. As a friend once told me: Marriage is not so much a matter of finding the right person as it is a matter of being the right person.

In the pages that follow, I am going to try to help you better understand yourself and your husband and learn to identify and seek solutions to the kind of problems that can lead to marriage breakdown.

I do not profess to have any miraculous cures for dirty socks, recurring ironing, or endless meal preparation. What I do have is a collection of clues, skills, and insights gathered from years of study, professional marriage counselors, and wives and husbands.

I want you to gain the feeling that you and your husband *can* affect what happens in your marriage. Together, you are in control.

As President Edmunds said, "Nothing is ever made that you do not make yourself." ("1,113 Couples, But How Many Marriages?" page 69.) So, while others may counsel and advise you, the ultimate decision of what to do is your own. No one else can make it for you. This really is your marriage.

Use this handbook to help you anticipate the joys and hardships, the normal ups and downs, and gain confidence in your ability to cope with and enjoy the years ahead. My purpose is much like immunization — a small dose to produce a mild case to prevent a catastrophe later.

For the most effective use of this information, you must always consider it from your own perspective. To facilitate doing this, I would suggest that you read it with a pen in hand, writing in the margins or wherever you feel inclined, noting whether you agree, disagree, or just question.

There is value in writing things down. As long as thoughts are loose in your mind, they remain shapeless and indefinite. But the effort of taking that idea and expressing it in specific words will greatly clarify your thinking.

Try it. I think you will find it works.

And don't be afraid to disagree with me. It does not mean that you are wrong and I am right. On the contrary, it probably means that you are aware of your own situation and have formulated some ideas about it. Your opinions have merit. Don't discount them until you have given them full consideration. The contents of this book may give you additional background against which to examine your ideas.

I know that no bride is going to retreat to a corner, curl up, and read this book from cover to cover right now — much as I wish you would.

Rather, I expect that, as with any other handbook, say for the car or curling iron, you will only refer to it as the need arises.

When you do, I hope that you will find the reassurance, the encouragement, or the help which you seek.

Marriage really is great. It's just like the proverbial bed of roses — sweet smelling and beautiful, though rather thorny at times.

2

The Bride

You are a bride! "Yes, at last," you sigh.

Are you happy? scared? excited? or too mixed up to know?

Perhaps the mixed-up feeling is partly due to the fact that, though there are definite traditions and ceremonies associated with *becoming* a bride, there are no such set guidelines for *being* a bride.

In fact, not even brides can agree totally on what they think it means to be a bride.

Most agree, however, that it has something to do with loving, cooking and cleaning, as well as budgeting, ironing, crying, decorating, having babies, and getting along with your husband, your in-laws, his in-laws, and . . . help!

The subject is so big. Does anyone know what a bride is?

I'm sorry to disappoint you, but I can't tell you exactly what a bride is. You see, while many functions are common to most brides, how you carry them out and how you feel about them differ with each girl.

Would you be willing to backtrack with me a little? I want each of you to be able to define your own role, functions, and goals.

Let's begin with the proverb, "A journey of a thousand miles begins with a single step." However overwhelming being a bride is, the first step is to learn what it involves.

Many years ago a family went from Canada to Salt Lake City to attend general conference and to see their older son, Bob, a student at BYU. The family drove down together, but the father, a doctor, had to fly home early.

Since it was Easter break, the mother and two younger children, ages fourteen and eight, stayed on to spend a few more days with Bob. All too soon it was time to start the long drive home, over a thousand miles through mountain passes and possible late spring snows. The mother was really worried. She didn't think she could manage the trip alone with the children.

A friend then told her, "Norma, you don't have to drive that whole eleven hundred miles at once. Just drive one mile at a time. You'll get home all right."

This new perspective changed her attitude immediately. Instead of being paralyzed by fear, she became calm and confident. She knew she could handle just about anything for one mile.

If you will take a major goal and break it up into small parts, eventually you will complete the whole.

This is a desirable kind of perspective for a new bride to adopt. Certainly the ultimate goal is to become a celestial wife. In the meantime, why not start by breaking that down into its parts?

The first small part is *you*.

This book is written to help you as an individual attain peace and happiness in your marriage. In order to really benefit from this material, you must know who you are, what you feel, and where you want to go.

As you look at yourself, try not to be overly harsh or critical: but be kind and honest. I do not think the Lord wants us to be haughty and proud, but he does not want us to put ourselves down.

He has created you. And he has also given you gifts to bring you and those around you joy (see D&C 46).

With this in mind fill out the following personal inventory.

Personal Inventory

Physically, I see myself as   a. attractive
                                      b. unattractive
                                      c. _____

Intellectually, I am
- a. very bright
- b. about average
- c. not very bright
- d. _____

Emotionally, I am
- a. secure, warm, and confident
- b. fine with people who like me
- c. insecure, lack confidence
- d. _____

Socially, I am
- a. friendly, outgoing
- b. reserved
- c. shy, withdrawn
- d. _____

Spiritually, I feel that
- a. the Lord comes first
- b. things come first
- c. religion is for the weak
- d. _____

I have
- a. a firm personal testimony
- b. an uncertain testimony
- c. no testimony
- d. _____

I believe the Holy Ghost is
- a. a real source of help and comfort
- b. a help to others
- c. imaginary
- d. _____

Personal prayer is
- a. a vital part of my life
- b. useful in a pinch
- c. for the weak
- d. _____

Things that I really like
- a. _____
- b. _____
- c. _____
- d. _____
- e. _____

Things that I do not like   a. _____
                                   b. _____
                                   c. _____
                                   d. _____
                                   e. _____

Things that I do well   a. _____
                                   b. _____
                                   c. _____
                                   d. _____
                                   e. _____

Things that I do not do well   a. _____
                                   b. _____
                                   c. _____
                                   d. _____
                                   e. _____

My favorite people are   a. _____
                                   b. _____
                                   c. _____
                                   d. _____
                                   e. _____

What is most important to me?   a. _____
                                   b. _____
                                   c. _____
                                   d. _____
                                   e. _____

What makes me happy?   a. _____
                                   b. _____
                                   c. _____
                                   d. _____
                                   e. _____

What makes me angry?   a. _____
                                   b. _____
                                   c. _____
                                   d. _____
                                   e. _____

What worries me?   a. _____

                                          b. _____

                                          c. _____

                                          d. _____

                                          e. _____

Skills which I have   a. _____

                                          b. _____

                                          c. _____

                                          d. _____

                                          e. _____

On the whole, I am   a. surprised and pleased

                                          b. pleased

                                          c. discouraged

                                          d. _____ with the

                                              results of this inventory.

Check one of these: ☐ I like myself.

                      ☐ I do not like myself.

Why?

The need to know and like yourself becomes apparent as you consider the second great commandment: "Thou shalt love thy neighbor as thyself." (Mark 12:31.)

I have always been impressed by the two parts of this commandment: love thyself; and love thy neighbor in the same way.

I have total and complete confidence in our Father in heaven. He knows you well, and he knows what you need to be happy. He gave this commandment because only as a person becomes confident and secure with himself can he reach out to others with love and acceptance.

Let me illustrate this. You are invited to a dinner party, but somehow you do not realize that it is a formal party.

On the night indicated you arrive, dressed comfortably in a sweater and skirt. All the other girls are glittering in long gowns and evening shoes. The fellows are in dark suits. There are even candles on the table.

Are you secure enough to forget about yourself while you try to draw the shy girl on your left into the conversation? Or would your reaction be more like: "Horrors! Look at me. Get me out of here."

This is perhaps a bit obvious, but few of us can reach out to others unless we feel comfortable about ourselves.

This leads into the next area of importance: self-image and self-esteem. You've heard these terms before, but do you know how greatly they can affect your life?

My husband and I had our three older children within a period of three years and nine months. That is not particularly unusual.

But I was afraid of children. As the youngest of a large family, I didn't associate with little people.

Later, when I walked to school, and this was high school, if there were youngsters playing on the sidewalk I would cross the street to avoid them for fear one of them might speak to me.

But suddenly I was with three preschoolers of my own. Much as I did love them, I was more than a little tense and insecure. The truth is—I was a lot tense and insecure. And though I felt competent in many ways, I started to emotionally unravel.

Just when I was ready to let them shovel the dirt over me, my perceptive husband gave me a book—a good way to reach a compulsive reader who reads even the backs of cereal boxes.

The book explained the practical application of psycho-cybernetics. More than anything else, the contents of this little book helped me to realize that I could become a competent mother if I did it to suit my personality instead of trying to match up to some Super Mom image.

I began to realize that, though what others think of you is important, the really crucial factor is what you think of yourself. Self-image is what you think of yourself.

Self-esteem is the result of a positive self-image. It is an emotional quality which has little to do with facts. As such, no one can prove to you that you have worth; rather, you must accept yourself and make a gift to yourself of it.

A reservoir of self-esteem is like a testimony. It can strengthen you and enable you to face whatever challenges may await you. Its value cannot be overestimated.

Yes, but how do I get it? Like every other good and true thing, it will only help you when you know how to apply it. Here, then, are ten specific ways in which you can boost your self-image.

1. Truly realize and accept that even if you are the second ugliest girl in the world, or the third most stupid, you still have worth because you are a person, a child of God. You were born with intrinsic worth which has nothing to do with looks, abilities, or desires.

2. In addition to this inherent value, God has given you bonuses in the form of specific gifts of the spirit (see D&C 46:11). Try to remember that a gift of patience or cheerfulness is every bit as valuable as the more visible gifts of singing or painting. In fact, in marriage the gifts of patience and cheerfulness might well be the best and most valuable ones.

3. Fast and pray for two things: to discover what your gifts are, and to be able to accept yourself and thereby release yourself from the web of self-abasement. Many of us have grown up with the idea that it is wicked to think well of ourselves. Let's separate haughtiness and pride from sincere but humble regard, respect and appreciation for qualities graciously given to you by your loving Father.

4. Pay attention to feedback from the significant others in your life. These are the people who mean the most to you — your husband, family, close friends and leaders. Do not get caught up in the opinions of those who are not important to you. If you hesitate too long at a freeway entrance and the driver behind you calls you a moron, don't file that in your mind. Let it go right by.

Do keep a discreet list of positive feedback from significant people. This can boost your self-image when you need it.

5. If you have ever received any awards or trophies, put these up where you feel the least competent: in the kitchen, over the ironing board, or by the sewing machine. It is a statement of, "I did that, so I can certainly do this."

6. Do something that you know you can do well. I have a friend who is tremendous in so many ways. She, like you and I, has some areas where she is not competent. If after Relief Society she hears her friends comparing notes on recent sewing successes, she feels a stab. She does not sew. If, instead of dwelling on her in-

adequacies, she will either whip up some sweet rolls or begin a new quilt, she will gain a feeling of satisfaction from performing her specialties.

7. Keep yourself looking your best by bathing frequently and by being well groomed and appropriately dressed—especially at home.

8. Help someone else without being assigned. Perhaps take a plate of cookies to the elderly couple down the street.

9. This is the opposite of number 8: Take time for yourself, without feeling guilty. As a Mormon woman, you may feel that it is more important to serve others than to take time for yourself. Actually, both are important, and both have their place. Anne Morrow Lindbergh speaks eloquently about this in her book *Gift from the Sea:*

> Is this then what happens to woman? She wants perpetually to spill herself away. All her instincts as a woman—the eternal nourisher of children, of men, of society—demand that she give. Her time, her energy, her creativeness drain out into these channels if there is any chance, any leak. Traditionally we are taught, and instinctively we long, to give where it is needed—and immediately. Eternally, woman spills herself away in driblets to the thirsty, seldom being allowed the time, the quiet, the peace, to let the pitcher fill up to the brim. . . .
>
> Even purposeful giving must have some source that refills it. . . . If it is a woman's function to give, she must be replenished too. But how? . . .
>
> Solitude, says the moonshell. Every person, especially every woman, should be alone sometime during the year, some part of each week, and each day. (New York, Random House, page 48.)

Mrs. Lindbergh goes on to say that if you really see the need for this solitude in your life, you will find a way to have it. I think she is right.

10. One final suggestion, quite elementary but effective, is to take a recipe card and cut it in halves. On each part, in your best hand, write "I am a person of worth" and tape one to your mirror where you will see it each morning as you straighten your hair, and put the other in your wallet. It will be there to give you courage when you need it away from home.

Thus far we have looked at being a bride as a major field which you can only come to grips with in small doses. Then we looked at you as an individual. After that, we emphasized the need for you to like yourself enough to fulfill the commandment "Love thy neighbor as thyself" and to develop some life-giving self-esteem.

Finally we are ready to talk about your role as a bride, then a wife and homemaker. This, as I've said before, can be quite complicated. I think the best approach is to start with a survey to see what you think you're expected to do in this new role you've adopted.

Make a comprehensive list of what you think you are expected to do as a wife and homemaker.

Great! Do you honestly expect to do all of that, for the rest of your life? If you try to emphasize too many things at once, you may be able to do only a mediocre job of all of them.

My question to you is, "How would it be if you were to consciously choose which things you think are the most important for achieving the kind of home you want?"

Would you be willing to do that? Go back to your list, study it carefully, even prayerfully, and select the ten things which you think would be most important for you to do regularly. List those things, and beside each, note the reason why you chose it.

Seeing these listed with the attendant reasons may cause you to change your mind. That is fine. Go ahead and do it. Just because you have written these down does not mean that you are locked into this pattern. Go ahead and revise the list as often as you feel the need, both now and throughout your life.

As circumstances change, so will your needs. Right now you do not need to set time aside to scrape porridge off the wall, but when you have a two-year-old, you will.

In a later chapter on home management we will return to this, so I would like to move on now. But before I do, there is one more thing I want to say to all you new homemakers: If you have an imaginary "Ideal LDS Woman" or a "Perfect Wife" or a "Super Mormon Mom" lodged in your mind, get her out of there right now!

She is so beautiful, so gifted, so competent, and so perfect, that no matter how hard you try, you will never feel good enough. She will constantly remind you what a failure you are because you do not measure up to her.

Get her out and replace her with a model of your own bent — the kind of woman that you have the talents, inclinations, and possibilities of becoming. You aren't sure who this woman is? Well, think about it. This is really the key to your success and happiness as a bride-wife-homemaker.

So, close your eyes, and try to visualize the kind of woman you really want to be. In as few words as possible, write down her major characteristics.

You now have a more realistic model after which to pattern yourself. She will enable you to be programmed for success instead of constant failure.

Aristotle is probably one of the first to have said, "What you expect, that you shall find."

That is why I think it is important for you to know what your goals — small immediate ones and larger long-range ones — are. Use these to build your life around in the best way you know how.

President David O. McKay once said, "The most sublime beauty and the greatest harmony in life are obtained when . . . the woman puts forth her best efforts along the lines for which she is best fitted." (Llewelyn R. McKay, comp., *True to the Faith*, Bookcraft, 1966, page 166.)

You are faced with the basic, flexible roles of wife and mother; now find the ways to fit these around you to take on your own beautiful and unique shape.

I have said enough, but continue to search your soul, talk with your husband, pray to the Lord, and find out how best to pursue your dreams and goals.

This is it. You've waited all your life for this — and now it's here. You are a bride. So find out what manner of bride you are to be and then do your best and enjoy it. You deserve to be happy.

3

Your Husband

"Your husband." Has a nice ring to it, doesn't it?

Do you really know who this man is? Oh sure, you know his name and his dimensions, *but who is he?*

Perhaps by now you have learned that the two of you do not agree about everything as you had hoped.

Remember what you told your mom and your friends when you first met him? "Oh, he's really something! He's so different."

Now after being married to him for a while, you are beginning to see just how different he really is. He doesn't like brown sugar in his stew; you have always had brown sugar in your stew. He wants his socks folded over four times and tucked into the cuff to make a ball; you have always only had the cuffs folded over. He leaves his dirty laundry on the bathroom floor; you had to put yours in the hamper or it didn't get washed. He sleeps with the window closed; you shut the window only when it got below freezing.

This list reminds you of some things of your own, right? Go ahead and write them down. While I don't want you to get "hung up" on them, I also realize that you can't just ignore them.

This all points to a basic truth. Every person is unique. In addition, you were born and raised in a family with its particular preferences, practices, and peculiarities. So now, along with your own individual differences, you each have a bunch of learned ones as well.

Is it any wonder, then, that the two of you do not see everything in the same way? The real wonder is that you do ever agree at all.

What attracted you to this fellow in the first place?

If you are shy, you may have been drawn to his friendly outgoing personality. Or, if you are a sit-and-watcher, it may have been his physical prowess that caught your eye.

In my opinion, the Lord may have planned for opposites to attract so that two divergent personalities could meet, complement each other, and make one whole. What do you think?

Let me use my husband and me as an example.

Hank is an intelligent, laconic, private person who has exceptional spatial aptitudes, loves physical activity, reads western novels for fun, and accepts life as it comes.

I am a high-strung, talkative, outgoing person who has strictly two-dimensional vision, hates all physical activity, reads only non-fiction, and is bent on changing just about everything.

You probably think I made this up. Actually it is a painfully true picture. About the only two things we have in common are the gospel and an instinct for the ridiculous.

For the first few years of our marriage, about the first twelve years in fact, I fought against some of his innate characteristics. I am a changer, remember. But, typically, he stayed loose, and over the years I learned to relax enough to see that the features in my husband which bothered me so much at first have become the very things for which I appreciate him the most.

Had he been as tense, easily upset, and anxious to change the world as I was, we would have driven each other into separate cells of the same institution. Both cells would have been padded.

But, as it was, his quiet, low-key approach to life complemented my frantic, volatile one, and we have become a couple — two people who retain our own individual identities but who also have learned to bend, adjust, and give in to each other enough to have become "one flesh."

Before we met, mutual friends kept trying to get us together. One in particular kept saying, "You and Hank need to get together. You're just like salt and pepper."

She was right. I'll leave you to decide which of us is the salt and which is the pepper.

So much for my husband. Now back to yours.

Try to see him for the individual that he is; not as a poor substitute for the man you wish he was. Some of you may be truly baffled by him because he is so totally unlike the fellow you dated.

This is not unusual since dating is often a masking game. After all, are you really the girl you seemed to be?

Now that you are married to him and your whole future is tied up with his, you had better get acquainted — really acquainted.

Some evening when the two of you are feeling mellow and totally accepting of each other, approach the subject. Ask him to tell you about himself so that you can get to know and understand him. Let him know that it will help you to appreciate him more; and be sincere.

Below is a profile chart from which you can get ideas for your discussion with him. Above all, do not make fun, or judge, or criticize, or belittle anything he says. Just listen. These are his feelings, and to him they are sacred.

How well do I know my husband?

Physically, I think he is
a. handsome
b. cute
c. striking
d. _____

Emotionally, he seems to be
a. secure, warm, confident
b. fine with those who like him
c. insecure, lacks confidence
d. _____

Socially, he seems to be
a. friendly and outgoing
b. reserved
c. shy and withdrawn
d. _____

Intellectually, he is
a. extremely intelligent
b. above average
c. average
d. _____

Spiritually, to him	a. the Lord comes first
	b. things are most important
	c. religion is for the weak
	d. _____
He has a	a. firm, personal testimony
	b. shaky testimony
	c. no testimony
	d. _____
To him, the Holy Ghost is	a. a source of help and comfort
	b. a helper to others
	c. an imaginary personage
	d. _____
To him, personal prayer is	a. a vital part of his life
	b. useful in a pinch
	c. for the weak
	d. _____
What he likes	a. _____
	b. _____
	c. _____
	d. _____
	e. _____
What he dislikes	a. _____
	b. _____
	c. _____
	d. _____
	e. _____
Things he does well	a. _____
	b. _____
	c. _____
	d. _____
	e. _____
What gives him trouble?	a. _____
	b. _____
	c. _____

d. _____
e. _____

His favorite people are

a. _____
b. _____
c. _____
d. _____
e. _____

His favorite foods

a. _____
b. _____
c. _____
d. _____
e. _____

What makes him mad?

a. _____
b. _____
c. _____
d. _____
e. _____

What makes him happy?

a. _____
b. _____
c. _____
d. _____
e. _____

Outside pressures he has

a. _____
b. _____
c. _____
d. _____
e. _____

What he expects from you as
his wife

a. _____
b. _____
c. _____
d. _____
e. _____

What he expects from himself
as husband

a. _____
b. _____

	c. _____
	d. _____
	e. _____
Does he feel secure in this new role?	a. yes
	b. no
	c. _____
What worries him about it?	a. _____
	b. _____
	c. _____
	d. _____
	e. _____

What is his ultimate goal in life?
Does he have self esteem?

Perhaps this outline will serve as a springboard for further discussions with your husband. In trying to gain this understanding now, you are establishing an all-important pattern: open communication, sharing thoughts, ideas, and expectations; facing problems, learning to cope instead of hiding them and pretending they don't exist.

Erase from your mind the false concept that differences will ruin your marriage. Differences, like problems, can be growth producing, depending upon your attitude toward them and your means of dealing with them.

Suppose you were planning a long weekend trip, and you found the car had a flat tire. You have two choices: stay home, or fix the tire and go.

The rest of this section will be based on the assumption that you are not a quitter. Here is a two-step system for utilizing differences to draw marriage partners closer together.

1. State the problem. Do not blame the other person, just describe what is bothering you.

2. Identify what the cause of the difficulty is, and try to reach some agreement on a solution.

Resolving differences is not easy, but the alternative makes it imperative that you acquire the skills needed. I will outline this and other systems in detail in the chapter on communication.

After devoting so many pages to underlining how unique your husband is, I now want to make some very general statements about him. This is dangerous because for every generality there are many exceptions. Still, I think there is value in looking at the following.

In general, most husbands like a wife who: is well groomed and cheerful; keeps an orderly and clean house; serves tasty food on time; stays within the budget and records all checks; keeps his clothes clean and in good repair; is quiet when he needs to study; has a testimony; is punctual and self-reliant; helps him feel good about himself.

In general, most husbands do not like a wife who: is totally helpless and dependent; plans every minute of the day and will not be flexible; assumes she knows what he is thinking; neglects basic housekeeping chores; forgets to record checks; is late for everything; has "hang ups" about sex which she will not discuss with him; gives him the silent treatment when she's mad; wants more than he can provide for; criticizes him both for what he does and what he does not do.

Husbands don't like being constantly corrected — it is both painful and humiliating, rather like being nibbled to death by a duck.

These are general likes and dislikes; some will apply to your husband and some will not. So start a file of specifics about your husband. It could save you many unpleasant and even painful encounters.

How he will feel toward you, and how he will treat you in all the years to come, will be a direct result of how you treat him. So, it makes sense for you to be as considerate of him as you can be.

How might you show consideration for your husband? I'm sure that after you read this list you will be able to add many more ideas of your own.

1. Love him unconditionally — that means even when he is late for supper.

2. Communicate openly with him about everything. He can be your very best friend.

3. Respect his need for privacy both at home and out. Never discuss your intimate lives with others.

4. Do not compare him to other husbands who may seem

smarter, more wealthy, better dressed, more athletic, or more spiritual.

5. Never belittle or ridicule his ideas, especially in public.

6. Do not compete with him to see who is right. This can lead to hard feelings and can kill what should be a warm, sharing, satisfying relationship.

7. Learn to present a united, supportive image to your families, friends, and later to your children. Discuss differences in private.

8. Know what his favorite things are. Does he like you to rub his back or his feet? Does he love chocolate cake, or apple pie, or liver? You can make a nothing day special for him by doing one of his favorite things.

9. Put on your nicest cologne at bedtime. He will know it is for him.

10. Do not go to your parents with your marriage problems. Stay home and work them out with your husband. One young wife comes to mind. She and her husband had experienced a number of disappointments, the most serious of which was the loss of their fourth child by miscarriage. She wanted to go to her parents, who lived thousands of miles away. But circumstances made this impossible. She felt badly.

In desperate need of reassurance and comfort, she turned to her husband who was also hurting. He responded magnificently and was able to offer her the reassurance and comfort which she sought. Both received strength from the other. The whole series of experiences reinforced their marriage with a deeper love. They are now closer than they have ever been before.

After the experience she remarked, "I found my peace with my husband, and I'm so glad, because I think that is where I'm supposed to get it."

Yes, girls, she is right. That is where you are supposed to get it. "Therefore shall a man leave his father and his mother, and shall cleave unto his wife; and they shall be one flesh" (Moses 3:24).

Now let's consider a final area of discussion: helping your husband to preside and fill his priesthood obligations.

In an LDS home the husband presides, whether he has the priesthood or not. You are his first counselor, but he is the president.

As his counselor your responsibility is to make recommendations based on your understanding, experience, and inspiration. Together you consider problems and look for solutions or look at opportunities and make choices.

Then he must make the decision. That is how the First Presidency operates. The counselors counsel and advise. They discuss. Then the president decides, prayerfully. Once the decision is made, the counselors support the president totally.

If you and your husband will follow this principle of presidency, you will have a peace born of the spirit of cooperation in your home.

Now, if your husband does have the priesthood, there is a further network known as "supporting your husband in his priesthood callings."

This means that your attitude and behavior can either help or hinder him in his Church work; to be supportive is to be helpful. How?

1. Have a strong personal testimony of your own.

2. Listen to him. He won't be able to share the confidences of his calling — so don't ask. But, he will need to share his triumphs and frustrations.

3. Recognize his efforts, and give him specific credit.

4. Encourage him by being extra helpful when he is under extra pressure. Express your faith in him.

5. Don't begrudge the time he spends filling his calling. This gets harder when you have little children. Sister Elaine Cannon told how she learned this lesson. She was waiting for her husband to come home for Sunday dinner. The dinner was getting cold, their four little children were cross, and so was she. Finally, she fed the little ones and put them down for naps.

As she continued to wait, she realized that her six-foot-six husband must be really hungry, and that if he could be, he would be home. She knew it had to be important, or he'd be home. Her attitude changed, and when he finally did come, she was able to greet him properly.

She told of how happy she was that she was able to be supportive when he told her why he had been so late. He had had an exceptional spiritual experience. She could have ruined it all if she had been cross when he came home.

If your husband should be called to accept a leadership position, you will have an even greater responsibility and opportunity. Let me just say one thing in this regard.

When he comes home after interviews, or a court, or a counseling session, give him time to unwind. Give him lots of emotional space. Do not meet him with demands of your own.

It takes a special kind of woman to be able to truly support her husband in his priesthood callings. When you are interviewed by the presiding authority as he prepares to call your husband to some responsible position, he will ask you if you are willing to support him in his prospective calling. What will you say?

This is a good place to leave you for now, thinking about this special man who is now your husband. This is not all there is to caring for and cultivating a fine mate, it is only the beginning.

4

Will the Marriage Fail?

While I was the Laurel adviser in our ward one of the girls stayed after a class on dating and marriage and asked, "Since marriage is a training ground for exaltation, doesn't it follow that for me to get the greatest benefit from it I should marry the most difficult man I can?"

I was speechless. Quickly she went on, "I mean, if I marry a really neat guy that I get along with, won't it be too easy? I wouldn't grow as much as I would if there were lots of problems to overcome. Would I?"

I could see that she was seriously considering the relationship between adversity and growth, and that was good.

But with a silent prayer and a pounding heart, I told her, "You marry the greatest, most considerate man you can. Even then, your marriage will present plenty of adversity to help you grow."

As we visited I tried to help her see that marriage is not a utopia where she would need to search for problems to overcome in order to precipitate her personal growth.

I was scared. What kind of Laurel leader could allow a beautiful seventeen-year-old girl to go out into the world with a misconception like that?

That conversation and many others like it have convinced me that we need to discuss marriage openly and realistically. To facilitate such a discussion, I have chosen these four areas:

1. What exactly is marriage?
2. Why do people marry?

3. Why do marriages fail?

4. Why do marriages succeed?

The first three follow here, while the fourth is covered in the next chapter.

What Exactly Is Marriage?

Marriage is the legal union of a man and a woman as husband and wife. The gospel of Jesus Christ enlarges on this concept considerably. "Marriage is a school in which we can learn cooperation, consideration, and conciliation." (*Family Relations*, The Church of Jesus Christ of Latter-day Saints, 1975-6, page 35.)

"Your marriage is a laboratory for Godhood." (*Achieving a Celestial Marriage*, The Church of Jesus Christ of Latter-day Saints, page 65.)

"Marriage is a union between two souls. It is a spiritual, intellectual, emotional, social, and physical union." (Reed H. Bradford, *Marriage and the Family in American Society*, BYU Press, page 5.)

So marriage is an all-encompassing relationship, the experiences of which can precipitate the individual growth and subsequent exaltation of both partners.

Sounds great, doesn't it? But, President Kimball warns, "Marriage is not easy; it is not simple as evidenced by the ever-mounting divorce rate." (*Marriage and Divorce*, page 11.)

Why Do People Marry?

As quickly as you can, list all the reasons why you got married. Nothing is too trivial to note.

Compare my reasons below with yours.

1. Living with a man without marriage, while widely practiced, is not acceptable to the Lord. Marriage is not merely a social custom, it is "ordained of God unto man" (D&C 49:15).

2. "Be fruitful, and multiply, and replenish the earth" (Moses 2:28). Marriage is part of the Lord's system for providing bodies and parents for his spirit children.

3. Celestial marriage is a requirement for eternal life.

4. Man and woman need each other. "The purpose of the union is to perfect and complete the nature of both souls." (Joseph

Fielding Smith, *Doctrines of Salvation,* 3 vols., Bookcraft, 1955, 2:43-44.)

5. Some people marry to overcome problems of loneliness, poor self-esteem, or even to escape from an unhappy home.

6. Marriage is an investment in two people by two people. It has the greatest potential return of any investment you can make. Note the words *potential return.* Nothing is guaranteed.

Why Do Some Marriages Fail?

There are millions of answers to this question. Think of the factors that could cause trouble in your marriage. List everything that concerns you.

Please understand that I am not cynical or pessimistic. On the contrary, I love the concept of perfection in marriage.

What I do not like is the unhappiness and guilt that overcomes people who think their marriages are doomed just because they have problems.

Perhaps one of the causes of marriage breakdown is that while couples want and expect maximum satisfaction, they do not know how to get it. Before you can find success in marriage, you need to recognize what causes failure.

The following are some factors which can prove troublesome in any marriage, even yours. I hope that by alerting you to them you may be able to prepare to cope with or avoid them.

The critical factor is for you to know that you are not at the mercy of circumstance. You can affect the direction of your marriage. You do have the power to act for yourself to either change the situation or to determine how it will affect you.

Before launching into the specific areas of possible conflict, think for a moment *why* problems arise in life.

One reason is that Heavenly Father has allowed us to experience challenges in our lives. "For it must needs be, that there is an opposition in all things. . . . It must needs be that there was an opposition; even the forbidden fruit in opposition to the tree of life; the one being sweet and the other bitter. Wherefore, the Lord God gave unto man that he should act for himself. Wherefore, man could not act for himself save it should be that he was enticed by the one or the other." (2 Nephi 2:11, 15, 16.)

Why does life have to have challenges?

Part of the answer lies in Hebrews 12:6: "For whom the Lord loveth he chasteneth." Then in D&C 122:4-7 there is a partial list of the kinds of trials you could face, plus the reason for them. They are to "give thee experience, and . . . be for thy good."

Comforting to know that, isn't it? And then we are told why it is necessary: "My son, peace be unto thy soul; thine adversity and thine afflictions shall be but a small moment; and then, if thou endure it well, God shall exalt thee on high; thou shalt triumph over all thy foes" (D&C 121:7-8).

So there it is. Trials are to strengthen you, and to exalt you, if you handle them well.

Here are the reasons for some failures in marriage:

1. Basic differences between the sexes.

"Man's love is of man's life a thing apart, 'tis a woman's whole existence." (Byron.)

2. Dissimilar expectations. Partners usually have different expectations. If you don't talk to each other about this, the unmet expectations of one or both may result in disappointment, hurt, anger, resentment, and finally war.

Also, many Mormon women have such high self-imposed expectations that no matter how well they do, they never quite measure up.

3. Poor homemaking skills. Tasteless food, unwashed socks, and a disorganized home are particularly serious because they cause daily irritations. Your situation may be further complicated by a mother-in-law who, after twenty-seven years of practice, can now make Mr. Clean look like a cleaning school drop-out.

4. Finances. You both may have entered marriage without realizing how much "two can live as cheaply as one" would actually cost. By the time you pay tithing, rent or mortgage, utilities, food, clothing, insurance, and all the rest, you are likely to have a problem.

5. Individual differences. I've discussed these before, but I can't just bypass them because they have the destructive potential of about eight tons of dynamite.

There are two major kinds: differences of preference and differences of principle.

The latter kind reach deep into a person to those things which matter the most to him. Religious beliefs fall into this category. As a rule, these differences are harder to negotiate for a satisfactory settlement than those related only to preferences.

6. Selfishness. This can spring up anywhere at anytime. Many things can trigger selfishness in even a seemingly mature person; such things as tiredness, illness, too much pressure, or a vague sense of being taken for granted can breed selfishness.

"The marriage that is based upon selfishness is almost certain to fail," says President Kimball. "Every divorce is the result of selfishness on the part of one or the other or both parties to a marriage contract." (*Marriage and Divorce,* page 22.)

7. Significant others. Unless the two of you live in complete seclusion, you are likely to experience some problems with the people outside of your marriage who mean a lot to you. These include parents (ever hear any of those awful mother-in-law tales) and other relatives and friends.

The Lord has counseled you, "Thou shalt love thy wife with all thy heart, and shalt cleave unto her and none else" (D&C 42:22).

8. Power struggles. There are people who feel they must be boss, causing negative feelings in those who are subjected to the bossing. This may start as simple competition and may seem harmless at first. Over time, however, always having a wife top his story, correct his facts, or find better solutions to problems, can make a man feel inferior, threatened, and defensive. He may even become indifferent to protect himself.

9. Lack of privacy. Marriage, being an intimate on-going relationship which offers no days off, can give rise to feelings of being trapped, or suffocated, or of losing one's own identity. This is particularly true where, in addition to normal adjustments, there are the added pressures of heavy studies, severe financial setbacks, differences of principle, or constant nausea.

10. Lack of communication. I considered putting a big red flag beside this one. I think that even minor differences can become major problems if a couple can't talk about them. Misunderstandings grow. The lack of communication is often at the base of many other marital problems like religious conflicts, money troubles, or sex-related problems.

11. Sex-related difficulties. As an LDS youth you were taught to avoid sex at any cost. Now that you are married sex is not only allowed but required; but you may still feel guilty or even embarrassed about it.

12. Inconsiderate behavior. For some unknown reason, the nice courtesies of courting are often shed at the marriage altar. One girl noted, "If I didn't recognize him, I'd have sworn that someone had replaced him just before the ceremony." In extreme cases lack of consideration is accompanied by verbal and even physical abuse.

13. Refusal to accept responsibility. When one or both partners refuse to accept responsibility for their behavior by constantly excusing themselves or blaming others, the relationship becomes unstable and unsatisfying.

Some young people go into marriage to escape from the responsibilities in their parental homes and are dismayed to find even greater responsibilities in marriage.

14. Lack of commitment, loyalty, or trust. Unless there is a strong sense of commitment or loyalty toward one another, a couple has little chance of staying united through the inevitable hard times of illness, financial reversals, lagging testimonies, or plain weariness. The problems that you do have should be faced and solved, if possible, in the privacy of your home. Do not carry problems to your mother, neighbors, or friends. If you sincerely try, but cannot reach a solution, talk with your bishop.

15. Boredom. A great misconception has run rampant throughout the history of the world, and people have been saluting it and believing it ever since. It is that "everybody else's life is more exciting and more satisfying than mine is."

Not true. Every life, no matter how glamorous or perfect it may appear, is largely made up of routine and tedium with occasional bright spots, just like yours. Homemaking routines do have one noticeable undesirable feature in that most of them self-destruct every twenty-four hours.

16. Lack of spirituality. Perhaps most serious of all the potential pitfalls is the tendency of couples to shut God out of their marriages. There was a lesson we used to teach the Laurels which showed marriage as an eternal triangle supported by pillars at each

point. These pillars were husband, wife, and God. If any one was missing, the marriage would be unstable. Failure to stay close to your Heavenly Father through regular daily prayer, fasting, repentance, and increased faith will aggravate every one of the other fifteen problem areas in marriage.

Sixteen pitfalls. Hopeless? Don't despair! It is unlikely that all sixteen will surface in your marriage, at least not all at once.

But, if any of them do surface, recognize them as normal marital turbulence which, if handled well, will enable you and your husband to level out for more smooth flying ahead.

I want to stress again that problems do not mean failure. Problems indicate life — a chance to learn, to grow, to adjust, and to be strengthened.

You already know that it is not the kind or amount of adversity you have which will shape your life, but rather what you choose to do with them.

Go on now and read the next chapter. It is a shopping list of positive and specific ways to avoid, overcome, or neutralize the many negative factors that we have just talked about in this chapter.

Marriage really is great, if you work at making it great.

5

Is Happiness in Marriage Possible?

Happiness in marriage is definitely possible.

Just before I was married a sister in the ward said, "Jeannie, marriage gets better every year. It improves with time."

I had not grown up in the Church and this was a totally new concept to me; I liked it. And after nineteen years, my husband and I agree that marriage does get better—but not automatically.

I sincerely believe that success and happiness are definitely possible for you if you know and believe it is possible for you and your husband, and if you are willing to work to make it happen.

This chapter is an itemized list of things you can do to build a successful marriage. This does not give a final solution but suggests samples to stimulate your thoughts as you seek for the particular things that will work for you.

As you read these pages consider, pray, and listen for the Holy Ghost. He can give you exactly the ideas you need.

To stimulate your thinking, consider the following ideas from a course on marriage in American society.

> Marriage is an experience that requires adjustment. Even though a man and a woman have many things in common, represent considerable maturity in their personalities, and love each other in an unconditional way, they need time to find the most acceptable ways of achieving a "Paired Unity" in which they can each continue to grow spiritually, intellectually, emotionally, and socially and at the same time complement each other. In some ways they have been conditioned to different types of behavior. (She likes to squeeze the tube of toothpaste in the center. He has been taught to roll the tube

from the bottom. She likes a house of order in which everything is in its place, but he has been conditioned to leave a thing or two lying around.) Therefore, it requires the following in order to reach the highest fulfillment in relating to each other.

(1) It requires sensitive concern for each other. This means that instead of feeling unduly upset when one's mate does something differently than you have been used to doing it you are willing to be patient.

(2) It requires a willingness to carry on a continued "dialogue" or communication with each other. The purpose of such a dialogue is to first try to understand each other and actually see if there are desirable behavior changes that should be made. If there are, the couple reaches a consensus on how this is to be done. (*Marriage and the Family in American Society,* page 29.)

Along with this beautiful concept, I would suggest that a good motto for a married woman is this well-known prayer: God grant me the serenity to accept the things I cannot change, courage to change the things I can, and wisdom to know the difference.

Even verbalizing or writing down the phrase, "Since there is nothing I can do about this, I am not going to worry about it" can help to relieve the tension.

Dr. Murray Banks, a prominent American psychologist, has said that every person has pressures and frustrations. But, he went on, it is not these pressures and frustrations that make people break down. Rather, it is their inability or refusal to adjust to them.

Then he added that adjustment is what you do to relieve tension or pressure. You may not be able to resolve a problem, but you can decide how it will affect you.

If you broke your leg, you could choose to complain and make yourself and everyone around you miserable, but you could not change the fact that your leg is broken. Actually, this type of reaction would greatly increase the distress of the injury.

Adjustment, on the other hand, would be demonstrated by your acceptance of the broken leg, the nuisance of the cast, and the restricted movement, and by trying to make the best of the whole situation. This attitude of accepting what can't be changed will not make the leg better immediately, but it will reduce the amount of distress felt by you and those around you.

The way you react to a problem is often more significant than the problem itself.

Some basic steps for successfully handling a stressful or annoying situation are to:

— identify the cause of the trouble.

— determine if there is any way you can correct the situation.

— decide what to do and then do it.

— decide to accept the problem and make the best of it.

— always maintain a repentant and forgiving attitude, toward both your husband and yourself.

How do you build happiness into your marriage? Here are some suggestions.

Basic Man-Woman Differences

Since male-female differences can't be changed, the best way to handle them is acceptance. You just expect your husband to think and react the same way you do. Dr. Carlfred B. Broderick of the University of Southern California advised: "Forgive him, if you can, for not knowing what you need, for not valuing what you value and for not seeing the need to repent of either. Feed him anyway; he may not deserve it but he badly needs it and will be far more likely to feed you back if he feels emotionally well nourished himself." (As quoted in a personal letter to author.)

Expectations

Share your anticipations about marriage, children, money, careers, and holidays with each other.

When you are next in charge of family home evening prepare a presentation on how your expectations differ.

You could use this illustration to introduce your lesson: Your husband expected to be paid forty dollars for a job. He was given twenty dollars. He was disappointed. Your husband expected to do a job for no pay. He was given twenty dollars. He would be pleasantly surprised. It was the same job. He received the same amount of money in both instances. The only thing that differed was his expectation, and it made all the difference in how he felt.

After presenting the illustration, discuss the importance of knowing one another's expectations about marriage. Hand out your two sheets and fill them in. Each of you write everything you can think of relative to what you want from your marriage and your life in general.

Look at your two lists together. Do not belittle, ridicule, or criticize one another's dreams and wishes, but do try to gain a real understanding of what is important to each of you. Understanding is what bonds two people together.

And just a few words about your own self-imposed, super-high expectations of having to be the perfect wife or the ideal home-maker. I strongly recommend that you get that perfection syndrome out of your head and replace it with a reasonable standard of your own which you can reach at least some of the time.

Perfection is the ultimate goal; but it is meant to help you reach and stretch, not to make you feel badly. Lift, not flatten, is the aim.

Homemaking Skills

Nearly every bride dreams of having a beautiful home. But the means to make it look that way are not usually part of the dream.

When you are first married and either working or going to school as well as keeping house, it is hard to know what is important and must be done, and what can be left undone.

Another good family home evening discussion would be to determine what will constitute essential services for your home at this time. Consider what other demands there are on your time, what is important to you both, what each of you are willing to do to help get the work done. Then try to agree on an acceptable standard.

In your first enthusiasm of being his wife, don't offer to do everything for him. (If you do, in six months or six years, you'll be sorry.) Rather, suggest that you help each other in the kitchen or in the traditionally male areas as the need arises.

If you are both able to be grown up enough not to evade doing what needs to be done when it needs to be done, you can work out a great cooperative system.

In our home the last person out of bed makes it; whoever is home when it snows clears it; if there are clothes that need folding, whoever can fold them does so. It is a supportive system which we both work to maintain.

Develop your basic homemaking skills — cooking and cleaning. Generally speaking, your husband will be happy if his wife can serve tasty food on time, keep an orderly home, and have clean clothes for him to wear. I would leave the extras for later when you have mastered the essentials.

Finances

Like expectations, the way to make money a unifying factor instead of a divisive one is to talk about it.

Find out how you each feel about money and what you'd like to use it for, and set up a budget which both of you are willing to stick to. This needs to be done early in marriage before financial tension becomes the established pattern.

Individual Differences

Differences of preference can add sparkle to your life. If his preferences are not too offensive to you, or matter but little, then just give in graciously. Try those exotic and weird things he learned to cook while on his mission — you might like them.

But if you feel strongly that you prefer not to go to another ball game but would rather go to a stage play or musical, tell him so, quietly. No tears, no accusations, no hysteria.

Joel and Audra Moss outlined a great system for resolving differences. It is the "Where are you on a scale from 1 to 10?" system. It is objective.

When you can't agree on what to do Friday night — you want to go to a movie, he wants to go to a ball game — ask, "How badly do you want to go to the game?" Then he asks you how strongly you feel about the movie. You both must be fair, and if you are the system will work. Whoever scores the higher number has the greater interest and the other should concede. You may devise your own way to settle differences.

Differences of principles are harder to negotiate. Perhaps you married a man whose basic beliefs and values are similar to your own. But, if you did not, you may soon find that love alone is not enough to neutralize deep feelings of what is and what is not important.

Do not suppress your true feelings just to keep peace. It will work for a while, but your real convictions cannot be denied forever without some cost. Ulcers are a common result.

It is healthier to admit there is a problem and open negotiations. If both of you will be honest, while showing sensitive concern for each other's feelings, you may be able to gain an understanding of one another's point of view. While you still do not agree, you will at least be able to continue to respect and love each other.

Making compromises in this situation is not a sign of weakness. In fact, there are times when trade-offs are a sign of great strength, love, and great wisdom.

When President A. Wood of the Alberta Temple was Deputy Minister of Lands and Forests in the provincial government, he often saw relatives disputing for the property of one who had died intestate. There was much contention and bitterness.

When individuals thus involved would go to him for counsel, President Wood would reply: "Sometimes the fight isn't worth it even if you are right. You stand to lose more than you'll gain and it just isn't worth it to tear the family apart for some property."

This advice is consistent with Genesis 12 and 13, which tell of Abram in the land of Canaan on the plains of Moreh which the Lord had given to him. Abram had Lot, his brother's son, with him as well. Eventually their individual flocks and herds became too numerous for the land to support them all.

The herdsmen of Abram and the herdsmen of Lot argued about who should go where. Remember, the Lord had given the land to Abram. He could have demanded his rights.

Instead, he said to Lot: "Let there be no strife, I pray thee, between me and thee, and between my herdmen and thy herdmen; for we be brethren. Is not the whole land before thee? separate thyself, I pray thee, from me: if *thou wilt take* the left hand, then I will go to the right; or if *thou depart* to the right hand, then I will go to the left" (Genesis 13:8-9).

Abram was unquestionably in the stronger position, but he

chose to graciously concede in order to maintain the relationship with his nephew.

It's true that if you never stand up for yourself you may get walked on a lot; but on the other hand, if you never give in you may become very rigid and unreasonable. The secret is in knowing when to stand firm and when to bend.

Mutual tolerance and fair play between your husband and yourself enables you both to know that it is safe to be understanding of each other. It will draw you together always.

Unfortunately, some of you will find that, in spite of all you do, your situation deteriorates and becomes intolerable. If this happens to you, go to your bishop. He will be able to advise you.

In this case, do not feel like a failure just because you need help. While it is important to be self-reliant in every way, it is equally important to be humble enough to know when you need help. Get it and follow it.

On a more positive note, one bishop who is a family counselor suggests that couples should consciously develop compatibility. For example, work at it by

—strengthening your own testimony.

—always being honest with him and yourself.

—listening to him, his feelings, worries, dreams.

—telling him your feelings, worries, dreams.

—letting him know you love and accept him as he is.

—working together: cooking, dishes, washing the car, gardening, painting and refinishing furniture.

—studying together: take a class, discuss current events at dinner, go to the library or museum, play your instruments.

—playing together: jog, walk, swim, ride together, play golf or tennis, do puzzles, play Scrabble, go on regular dates.

—doing spiritual things together: take an institute class, attend meetings together, work on histories and genealogy, go to education week.

You married this fellow so you could be together, didn't you? Now, find ways to enjoy and enrich that togetherness. If you patiently work at compatibility, you will find that he can be your best friend as well as your husband.

Don't let your differences pull you apart, use them to advantage for variety and spice — an antidote for boredom.

Selfishness

"The natural man is an enemy to God" (Mosiah 3:19), and selfishness is part of the natural man. If one is so self-centered that he does not care about others, selfishness is extremely destructive. But each woman needs to have a basic regard and respect for herself or she will find it hard to serve others.

"Love thy neighbor as thyself" (Mark 12:31). You have to love yourself, and then give that kind of love to others.

Do something nice for yourself every day and then forget about yourself and concentrate on the needs of those around you.

Treat your husband in a way that will keep telling him that he is special to you. Quit worrying that you are giving more than he is. Marriage is not a fifty-fifty arrangement. It needs to be a one hundred-one hundred arrangement. Don't hold back; give your all and your partner will most often return the generosity.

Try
— listening to him, really paying attention when he talks to you.
— laundering his jeans the way he likes them.
— cooking his favorite foods whenever you can.
— asking for his opinion on things — first, before your mom or girl friend.
— respecting his need for privacy, or time to study.
— feeding him first when he comes home, saving problems for later.
— not finding fault with his every effort, encouraging him.
— going to his parents' home for Christmas.
— forgiving him readily as you would like him to do for you.
— appreciating what he does for you, and telling him so.
— recognizing his good qualities and telling him.
— encouraging him to fill his Church callings well.
— accepting his preferences in food, clothes, reading material.
— laughing at his jokes, even if he's told them before.
— being ready for meals, Church, and dates on time.

—never taking him for granted.

—reminding yourself of what he gave up to marry you.

—being humble, praying always, enjoying your husband.

President Kimball said, "Love, also, cannot be expected to last forever unless it is continually fed with portions of love, the manifestation of esteem and admiration, the expression of gratitude, and the consideration of unselfishness." (*Marriage and Divorce*, pages 22-23.)

Privacy

It's great to be married. It's great to be together. But you are still individuals and as such will still require some time alone. Everyone needs privacy, a time to totally let down all the defenses and be completely relaxed. Your husband needs that. You need that.

Various psychiatrists and counselors call this the need for psychic space or emotional space—room to unwind. Call it what you like, but make allowances for it in your marriage.

Do not insist that he share every hour, every dollar, every thought with you. Men have been known to become secretive and devious in order to have one little corner of their lives totally to themselves. Don't force him into that.

If he loves to ski, but you really can't tolerate it, encourage him to go with one of his old buddies who also loves to ski. It will refresh you both. Or, if he likes to go fishing, don't sulk because he is going out to do what he loves; plan to do something you love to do while he is away.

You both need to have some areas of your lives that do not just mesh together. One can sweeten the other.

And leave his razor alone!

Significant Others

No matter how close you were to your parents before marriage, things have changed now. You are a married woman. Your first allegiance belongs to your husband, not to your mom and dad.

Dr. Broderick advises, "Don't let your parents or in-laws define the relationship; you and your husband need to set the limits, establish the tone, and control the interaction."

Important decisions must be reached by the two of you. Your parents may advise, but the decision must be yours. Sorrows and disappointments, too, must be faced as a couple.

Power Struggles

Marriage is a partnership where you are both working for the same end. It is not, therefore, a competition.

It can be a wonderful relationship which is uplifting and rewarding to you both if you will build each other up instead of struggling to dominate each other. The following are suggestions on achieving this:

— maximize his virtues, minimize his faults
— always be courteous
— do not order one another around; make suggestions or requests in a considerate way
— do many things yourself instead of trying to get him to do them because you think they are *his* jobs
— give him credit for the things he does; be appreciative
— cooperate; put the needs of the marriage ahead of your own
— admit when you are wrong
— encourage him in all he does; be supportive instead of critical
— never put each other down, not even at home

I've observed couples where the two try to outdo each other. They correct each other's facts, ridicule each other's ideas, and compete for the attention of friends. Love cannot grow in an environment like that. It eventually is replaced by indifference or hostility. No one wins in a power struggle in a marriage.

Communication

Talking to one another is so important to the stability of a marriage that the next chapter is devoted to it.

The following are the basic parts of good communication:

— send clear messages; know what you mean, then say it
— do not combine the idea of the message with the personality of the receiver; do not attack

—describe what is bothering or pleasing you; do not judge
—receiving is as important as sending messages, so learn to listen for verbal messages and watch for nonverbal ones
—share your real feelings; do not play games
—express positives often rather than negatives only
—*never* assume that you know what your husband is thinking or what he is about to say, wait and let him tell you
—do not sulk and say, "You'd know what I need without me telling you, if you really loved me"; he's not a mind reader

Sex-related Problems

Sex in marriage is not sinful when it is kept within the proper bounds. President Joseph F. Smith said, "The lawful association of the sexes is ordained of God, not only as the sole means of race perpetuation but for the development of the higher faculties and nobler traits of human nature, which the love-inspired companionship of man and woman alone can insure." (As quoted in *Achieving a Celestial Marriage*, page 78.)

Fears, lack of knowledge, or "hang-ups" about sex are common. If you have some, discuss them with your husband.

Some brides are concerned because their husbands seem much more interested in sex than they are. If the Lord had not given men such a strong drive, they might never have committed themselves to marriage. This is another basic male-female difference about which you can do nothing; just accept it.

Many girls also worry that if they don't experience orgasm each time, they are frigid. That is nonsense. Talk to your husband and your doctor about it. Relax, and quit worrying that you are a failure. You'll be fine.

But if you continue to find the experience painful or unpleasant, see a gynecologist. Or, if the problems increase, talk with your bishop.

But don't give up, because a satisfactory sexual relationship is very important to a good marriage.

Remember to

—keep yourself fresh and clean.
—splash your nicest cologne on at bedtime; he'll know it is just for him.

—wear your pretty things at home.

—make consideration for your hairstyle always second to your consideration for him.

—avoid sticky, greasy preparations on your face at night; they are not appealing, and they'll stain the bedding.

—go ahead and snuggle up to him. It will be good for his ego; he has insecurities, too.

Inconsiderate Behavior

Treat your husband as if he were the most precious person on the earth. Because to you he is—or should be. Show him every consideration. Among other things this means

—be sincere, do not "sweetheart" him with your teeth clenched.

—be punctual, don't keep him waiting.

—be generous with positive, encouraging remarks.

—give him some privacy.

—be tactful and gentle when something is bothering you.

—use "please, thank you, excuse me" and other words that show your high regard for him.

—meet him at the door with a smile and a kiss.

—see him off the same way.

—send his suits to the cleaner regularly.

—celebrate his birthday the way he wants it.

—think of him first, you second.

In marriage, the little things are the big things.

Accepting Responsibilities

When things go wrong

—do not make excuses.

—do not automatically blame someone else.

—ask *what* happened, not *who* did it.

—if you are wrong, admit it.

—zero in on the cause of the problem. ("The bank called to-day. They have checks clearing that are not recorded in our check book.") Just state the problem, do not blame or make excuses.

—be willing to help find solutions.

—brainstorm together looking for possible solutions; nothing is too impractical when you are at the first stage of problem-solving.

—together choose what you agree is the best solution and do it with all your heart to make it work.

To live responsibly and in harmony, accept problems at face value. Don't worry about whose fault it is, but seek the best solution and work together at overcoming the difficulties. Then you will begin to consider ways to avoid similar kinds of troubles in the future. You begin to act instead of reacting, and that is a good position to be in.

When your husband does act in a responsible way, acknowledge it, simply and directly: "I'm really glad you changed that tire. Now I won't be afraid to use the car. Thanks."

Loyalty and Commitment

The marriage relationship is a sacred one as well as a legal one. It requires total commitment of the "no matter what, I am sticking with it" variety.

Marriage can be difficult, but you must give your husband 100 percent of your love and loyalty. He needs to know that you accept him, faults and all. He needs your support and encouragement to give him the courage to become the man he is capable of being.

When trials come, leaving the marriage should never be one of the alternatives you consider. Work together in a responsible way to cope with the trials. Do not call in your parents or the neighbors. This is your private life.

I have said very little about love in this book, but I have concentrated on the ways to manifest your love. You see, just saying "I love you" is not enough. You must show your love in the way you treat him, meet your responsibilities, and live and feel from day to day. Love takes time, it takes effort, it takes accepting the good times as well as the rough times, and it takes total loyalty.

Do not let your eyes rove to any other man. Never allow yourself to be in a situation where you might be tempted. Be conscious of fidelity. Do not give your husband cause to seek comfort and sympathy elsewhere. Be his sweetheart every day so he will always be anxious to come home to you. If you do this, he is not likely to ever break his trust with you.

This is your marriage. It can grow into a celestial marriage. Be united and work together to keep all the commandments, and be happy so you can spend all eternity together.

Boredom

Almost anything is interesting once, or even twice. But for it to stay interesting for twenty-nine days, or seven years, or forever, is asking a whole bunch, isn't it?

And yet, that is precisely what you expect from marriage. Be realistic and recognize that a certain amount of boredom is inevitable. Then plan to do what you can to keep it at a minimum.

My husband places a lot of emphasis on what he calls "nothing days." Nothing days are all those ordinary days which separate the few special days of the year. Nothing days are the days when it is not Christmas, Easter, July the Fourth, somebody's birthday, payday, or the International Steeple Chase Championship.

Hank has helped us to keep these days from being dull, dull, dull. Fortunately, his philosophy and wisdom have rubbed off on us.

I recall one very warm, ordinary Saturday many years ago. We took the children to the city market to pick up bedding plants, cleaned the back yard, went to the zoo, and then to a Church picnic. On the way home we stopped for frozen treats.

Finally, as we backed into our driveway at sunset, I turned to the dusty little people in the back and said, "Well, we've had a real day today, haven't we?"

I'll never forget the little voice of Karen, then only six, as she emphatically stated, "*Every* day is a real day, mom."

She had spoken a truth, and I will always remember it. Here are some ways you can enjoy all the nothing, real days of your year. Jot down any other things that come to your mind as you read these.

— Develop an attitude that fun can be had at home for no cost; get rid of that notion that you have to go out to have fun.
— Serve a special breakfast on your brightest cloth some cold, dark winter morning.

—Tape a note to the middle of the bathroom mirror with a new toothbrush attached: "Happy 276th day of the year: I love you!"

—Slip his favorite candy bar into his coat pocket.

—Hide a new novel or cartoon feature in the bed, right where his feet will touch it when he goes to bed. This is for when he can sleep in the next morning. The cartoon book is fun because you two can lie there and laugh until you cry.

—Go on a three-dollar date where you must spend exactly three dollars.

—Build up a collection of games and puzzles.

—Give him some fun coupons to redeem whenever he chooses.

—Paint the bathroom together—crowded but fun.

—Listen to the oldest records in your collection.

—Have an elephant joke marathon.

—Go to the genealogical library together.

—Browse through a seed shop.

—Invite your favorite older couple in for dessert.

—Dress up to go out for dinner, set the table as for company, write a note of "I love you because," and then fix and serve him his favorite meal.

—Keep your sense of humor, look for the fun in life.

—Take pleasure in little things.

Married life shouldn't be boring. This is the fellow you went out with to have a good time, remember?

Keep the Lord in Your Marriage

The Spirit of the Lord can add a dimension to your relationship which you can get in no other way. Cultivate and nurture this spirit in your home every day:

—Pray together morning and night.

—Have your own personal prayers twice daily, at least.

—Make time for daily scripture study, either together or individually.

—Read the Church publications, especially the messages of the First Presidency.

—Attend Sunday meetings regularly together.

—Take an institute class.

—Work on histories and genealogy.

—Keep your journal up to date.

—Accept and fulfill Church callings.

—Go to the temple often.

—Be a friend.

Don't worry that you can't do everything all at once. The Lord understands and he *"seeth* not as a man seeth; for man looketh on the outward appearance, but the Lord looketh on the heart" (1 Samuel 16:7).

As a Latter-day Saint bride, you may feel that so much more is expected of you than of your nonmember friends, and you are right. Remember, too, that you have an added strength that few others can even understand, let alone share until they too take on the higher expectations the gospel brings. Utilize this spiritual force to the full. It will bring you great rewards — ultimately, a celestial marriage and exaltation.

What will your marriage bring you?

It will bring some days of happiness, some days of misery. But the days of happiness will more than compensate for the days of misery.

Know that you do have the power to act and to affect the quality of your life together. Be positive, expect to succeed; then work and pray hard to have it come true.

"The Lord asks us to believe we can do it, look to him for blessings, make the sacrifice, expect a miracle, and then receive it with humility," says Elder Hartman Rector, Jr. ("Following Christ to Victory," *Ensign,* May 1979, page 29.)

Yes, happiness in marriage is possible. It is possible in *your* marriage.

6

Communication

"I know that you believe you understand what you think I said, but I am not sure you realize that what you heard is not what I meant."

Communication is not a new concept to you. Ever since you were a baby you have been communicating by use of signals, sounds, speech, or writing. So, why am I doing a chapter on it here?

There are several reasons: As with other things, just because you know how does not necessarily mean that you can do it effectively; the difference between effective and noneffective communication skills is slight, but the difference in the results is tremendous; ineffective communication can get you into trouble; effective communication can enrich your life; effective communication skills can be learned.

By definition, communication is the exchange of thoughts and feelings between two or more people. One sends the message, another receives it. Only when the receiver gets the same message as the sender sent has effective communication occurred. When the sender sends one message, but the receiver gets a different one, the result is a miscommunication or a misunderstanding.

Why Is Communication Important?

Human beings have thoughts and feelings which give rise to basic human needs. Among these is the need to feel important to oneself and others.

John Dewey, an American philosopher, said, "The deepest urge in human nature is the desire to be important. It is a gnawing, unfaltering hunger. People sometimes become invalids in order to win sympathy and to get a feeling of importance. Some authorities declare that people may actually go insane in order to find, in that dreamland of insanity, the feeling of importance that has been denied them in the harsh world of reality." (As quoted by Vaughn J. Featherstone, "The Impact Teacher," *Ensign,* November 1976, page 103.)

Closely connected to this is the need to feel loved and accepted by others. But without communication, every person would be isolated and these needs could not be met.

This statement by George Eliot expresses the essence of what communication means in human relationships. "Oh, the comfort, the inexpressible comfort of feeling safe with a person; having neither to weigh thoughts nor measure words, but to pour them all out, just as they are, chaff and grain together, knowing that a faithful hand will take and sift them, keep what is worth keeping, and then, with the breath of kindness, blow the rest away." (Charles Wallis, *The Treasure Chest,* New York, Harper & Row, 1965, page 702.)

That kind of understanding is a worthy goal in marriage. President Hugh B. Brown, in his book *You and Your Marriage,* said, "Just 'talking things over' goes far toward reaching a solution. It keeps the couple in rapport, but if the line of communication between husband and wife is severed, by sulking, or temper tantrums, what was once exuberance and joy give way to indifference, misunderstanding, and, if not corrected, active dislike and hatred." (Hugh B. Brown, *You and Your Marriage,* Bookcraft, 1960, page 30.)

Good communication is essential, especially in a close marriage relationship. Therefore, some basic guidelines in sending and receiving messages would be helpful in making communication more effective in your home.

Receiving Messages

Many people think that receiving messages requires no conscious effort. This is not true.

"We confuse hearing with listening, believing that, because hearing is a natural function, then listening must be effortless. According to an American speech communications expert, Dr. Harrel T. Allen, it is anything but: 'Listening is hard work and requires increased energy—your heart speeds up, your blood circulates faster, your temperature goes up.' " (The Royal Bank of Canada Monthly Newsletter, January 1979.)

Here are some hints on improving your listening skills:

—Pay close attention, maintain eye contact.
—Encourage your husband to keep talking; respond, and show that you are interested in what he is saying.
—Develop an attitude of wanting to understand what he says and how he feels.
—Summarize what you think you are hearing to make sure you are getting the message straight.
—Reflect the feelings you see being expressed along with the verbal message.
—Offer help and encouragement.
—*Do not* evaluate, judge, disapprove, contradict—just listen.
—*Do not* show power or superiority and give your solution to his problem, unless he requests it.
—*Do not* belittle, ridicule, put down, or attack in any way.

Good listening is necessary for gaining understanding. An especially good technique is called reflective listening, which is a sensitive, concentrated kind of listening where you try to identify the feelings, the frustrations, fears, disappointments, happiness, or sorrow that the other person is experiencing. As you recognize what feelings he seems to be having, you reflect these back to him; he then can correct you if you are missing the point.

Husband: "Boy, one of these days I'm going to tell that boss of mine to take a one-way trip to Siberia!"

You: (Don't say, "You shouldn't talk about your boss like that. It isn't nice." He is entitled to his feelings. See if you can correctly identify how he feels.) "You seem upset."

Husband: "I'm upset all right. Do you know what he told me today? He said that I have to work the midnight shift for three weeks running. Two weeks is bad enough. Now he wants me to work three. Well, he can go jump in the lake!"

You: "That seems unreasonable to you."

Husband: "Yes, it does. He sure has his nerve. I've half a notion to quit."

You: "You really feel he's being unfair."

Husband: "I sure do. I wonder how he'd like it if he had to leave his wife alone every night. I'd rather stay home with you, you know. In fact, Geoff mentioned that their plant is taking on men. Maybe I should check with him; what do you think?"

You: "Sure, I'd love to have you home nights. That would be great."

Husband: "Yes, it would. You know, I think I'll call Geoff right now."

Too perfect? Sounds like the lines from a play? Well, at first it feels very phony, but the more you use it, the more natural it becomes. And, it really does work.

When a person is allowed to express his strong feelings and is accepted anyway, the anger dissipates. Too often the listener contradicts him, and further anger is felt. Then a fight begins. He's already upset, he doesn't need you putting him down, too. You're his wife.

The ideal result of reflective listening is for the one with the problem to be able to talk freely in an accepting atmosphere until he thinks of a solution himself.

Even if you don't reflect back accurately, it will still work because he can correct you as you go along. Stay alert.

Husband: "I'm swamped—beat. This job is really getting to me."

You: "You feel like quitting."

Husband: "No, not exactly. We have a new boss, too."

You: "Your new boss is tougher than Mr. James was?"

Husband: "Not really. He's all right, I guess."

You: "You feel unsure of yourself with him? You haven't gotten used to him yet?"

Husband: "Well, they've reclassified my job, too, you know."

You: "So you feel pretty pressured."

Husband: "Well, yeah, I guess that's it. But, I guess I'll give it a couple of weeks and see if it settles down any."

So, if you get it wrong, it can still work out to help him think out the situation. This is why reflective listening is so valuable. It increases understanding.

To help you remember how important it is not to judge, contradict, or criticize in reflective listening, think of this from Dr. Haim G. Ginott, "From a mirror one wants a reflection, not a sermon." (*Between Parent and Child,* New York, Avon Books, 1969, page 40.)

You don't need to agree or disagree; you just need to listen and try to understand his position.

Sending Messages

The other part that's required for communication to take place is to send messages. Talking comes easily for many people, but there are a few rules that will help to make your talking, or message sending, more effective:

—Know what you mean before you start to talk.
—Say what you mean as clearly as possible.
—Mean what you say, do not play games.
—Coordinate your verbal and nonverbal messages so they are the same.
—Do not put down, judge, criticize, command, attack, or blame.
—Send lots of positive messages.
—Send negative messages in a nonattacking way.
—Be honest with yourself and your husband.
—Always try to keep his self-worth intact.

In any given week, you may send hundreds of messages. They probably all fall into one of these general categories: messages of information; messages that ask a question; messages that praise; messages of encouragement; messages you send when you are upset; messages you send when you are both upset (some call this arguing, fighting, bickering); messages of support.

Messages of information. Just *describe* what you want to say. Do not evaluate, blame, or make excuses. Keep it simple. Say, "I burned the potatoes. Sorry," instead of, "That stupid stove: It's impossible to cook decent potatoes on it." Or, "I'm going to fill the gas tank today," instead of, "I suppose I'd better buy gas today or one of these days I'm going to get stranded on the freeway. How come you never fill it?"

Messages of question. Stick to the question, do not presume you know the answer. Do not whine. The tone of voice can wreck an otherwise good question. Ask the question directly instead of hinting around. Ask the question that is on your mind, not a decoy. Say, for example, "Are you going home teaching Wednesday night?" not, "Can we go to the movie Wednesday night or do you have to go home teaching?"

Messages of credit and praise. Be sincere, never flatter. Be specific, refer to one specific event or situation. Do not overdo it, do not gush. Keep the action separated from the personality, avoid the good boy, bad boy comments. Be generous, give praise often, whenever it is deserved. Remember that the purpose of credit is to build self-esteem. You are evaluating the action or event, not the person.

Most people are embarrassed by heavy praise, so keep it simple. If your husband gets a good hit in a ball game, say, "That was a great hit. I'm proud of you," rather than "You're such a great player."

If you praise the action, there is no let down when he doesn't do as well the next time. But, if you praise him, his worth seems dependent upon his performance. That can be threatening.

Dr. Ginott wrote the following statements, which may help you remember the elements of non-threatening praise: "Praise, like penicillin, must not be administered haphazardly." "The single most important rule is that praise deal only with the [person's] efforts and accomplishments, *not* with his character and personality." (*Between Parent and Child,* page 45.)

Messages of encouragement. Messages of encouragement are similar to messages of praise. They show your trust and faith in him as well as that you recognize that what he has to do is difficult. They give him an "I can do it" feeling and let him know that you love him, regardless of what happens.

When your husband has challenges he's not sure he can handle, it is your place to give him encouragement and support. Everyone has doubts. It doesn't mean he is weak but that he is human. What you say and how you act can make a big difference in how he sees and feels about himself.

If he has been out of work for several weeks and is going to another interview, how will he feel if you say: "I hope you get the job this time. We sure need the money. I hate having to scrape pennies like this."

Try saying, "I know you will give your best at this interview. Remember I'm pulling for you and that I love you, job or no job."

If he's going to a particularly difficult exam which he is worried about, don't put him further on the spot by saying, "Not to worry, you're so smart you'll ace it for sure."

You can help him feel more relaxed with a comment like this: "This one is going to be hard, isn't it? But you have worked hard, so it should come out all right. I'll be praying for you."

In the first examples, if he fails he loses more than a job or a passing grade, he loses self-respect and esteem. You have put him in a position where failure means a loss of your regard for him. In the second examples, you have not applied that kind of pressure. Instead, you have recognized the difficulty and have pledged support, no matter what. That is encouragement. That is security. That is what he needs.

Messages you send when you are upset. Reflective listening is what you do when he is upset, but when you are upset you need a new system. Many girls cry when they are upset. When a concerned husband says, "What's the matter?" the answer is often a muffled, "Nothing."

That may be dramatic, but it isn't very good communication. It does nothing to help solve the problem that has you upset.

Perhaps you've been taught all your life to hide your feelings, to keep smiling and pretend that everything is rosy. When you are afraid, angry, confused, disappointed, furious, humiliated, hurt, scared, or just plain upset, you should tell your husband about it. Pushing it down will not make the bad feeling go away.

Negative feelings should not be fed and cultivated, but they are bound to arise in a relationship that is as close and constant as marriage. Rather than covering them up because you feel such thoughts are unworthy, accept them, face them, and get rid of them. You are not a bad person because you occasionally have negative feelings toward your husband. Your marriage isn't going to fail if you disagree with him at times.

It is important to learn how to handle those negative feelings in an acceptable, nonattacking way. Remember it is not the problem that can wreck your life, it is the way you handle it. "Absence of conflict does not bring happiness, and that conflict in and of itself is not bad, but is normal. The number of conflicts in a family does not indicate a lack of spiritual or emotional health. Rather, *the key to happiness is simply whether or not the conflicts are resolved,* and how." (LDS Social Services Parent Education manual, page 1-1.)

So the question is, how should you handle your conflicts? The LDS Social Services parent education course has outlined a system which I think is the answer. It is what I call the *fabu*lous system for expressing negative feelings in a nonattacking, constructive way.

Simply, this system contains the following statement, which is to be used in stressful situations: I *feel* worried (confused, annoyed, upset, etc.) *about* (whatever situation you are talking about) *because* of how it affects me.

Suppose your husband had promised to have the spare tire repaired and put back in the car. He did not, and you had a flat tire on the freeway during rush hour. The week's groceries were in the car, and you had to accept a ride with a stranger to get home. The car and groceries are still out on the freeway. You probably have some negative feelings. What should you do?

Fit your feelings into the FAB formula.

"I *feel* furious *about* there being no spare tire in the car *because* today I had a flat tire on the freeway during rush hour, and not only was it humiliating and inconvenient, but the car is still out there with our groceries in it."

You have shared your feelings in an objective and complete way which should leave no room for him to misunderstand what it is that has you upset. You have not called him any names, you have not blamed him, you have just stated what has happened and how it affected you.

Perhaps you could just have smiled, shrugged the whole thing off, and acted as if nothing had gone wrong. But you can be totally honest about negative feelings and still not attack the other person. At first it might feel like you are reading lines from a B movie, but with practice it can become your greatest communication tool.

This system also works beautifully when you are pleased, happy, surprised, excited, or proud. It is great for giving specific praise.

When the car is once more complete with four tires and a good spare, you could express your appreciation: "I *feel* happier *about* using the car *because* I am not likely to get into a tight situation with it. Thanks for fixing it. It means a lot to me."

Messages sent when you are both upset. When you are both upset at the same time, you are in conflict. Again, don't shudder and try to hide conflict for fear that it means you are not a good Latter-day Saint. "The so-called 'ideal' family lives happily, not because it is lacking in conflicts, but rather because it faces them openly and resolves them. . . . Happy families struggle with and resolve conflicts." (LDS Social Services Parent Education manual, page 1-1.)

"Therefore, if ye shall . . . desire to come unto me, and rememberest that thy brother hath aught against thee—Go thy way unto thy brother, and first be reconciled to thy brother, and then come unto me with full purpose of heart, and I will receive you." (3 Nephi 12:23-24.)

And further, it is good to remember that "true peacemakers do not try to hide their problems, they resolve them." (LDS Social Services Parent Education manual, page 7-15.)

How then, do you resolve conflicts so they produce growth instead of heartache? Consider the following ideas:

—Identify and talk about the problem (FAB).
—Listen to each other (reflect).
—Understand one another's points of view (you do not have to agree).
—Plan and brainstorm to find possible solutions to the problem.
—Choose one of the solutions and determine how and when to put it into action.
—Check it out with the Lord (see D&C 9:8-9).

—Act on the decision.

—Evaluate the progress at a set time (deadline).

—Strive to be united.

Follow-through or evaluation is very important. This is easily forgotten unless you have a set time when you meet to do it. We find that family home evening is a natural time for this. You can brainstorm one week and come up with a decision; the next week do the follow-through. Do not neglect the follow-through.

Let me urge you once more to try and establish an open attitude towards conflict in your life. Learn to face and resolve conflicts so they produce growth and closeness, strength and appreciation in your marriage. Even a small problem, if it is never addressed, can continue to fester and cause contention for years. A very major problem, on the other hand, can actually draw you together if you face it and work to resolve it.

Finally, there is the underlying matter of being supportive of one another. A supportive spouse will accept errors rather than blame the other and encourage him to lose self-esteem.

Sometimes husbands and wives are so insecure in themselves that they say harsh and destructive things. "I told you so," "If you would ever listen to me you wouldn't have so much trouble," or "Can't you ever do anything right?" are the kinds of comments that put your spouse in a position of being wrong no matter what. It creates a sense of hopelessness, of defeat and unhappiness. Being super critical and nonsupportive in marriage is self-defeating. It hurts both of you.

Miscommunications, misunderstandings, and nonsupportive communications cause pain, whether between friends or family, but particularly between husband and wife.

Nonverbal Messages

Regardless of what kind of message you send, be aware that along with the words spoken there is another very powerful means of communication—nonverbal communication. "The look on a man's face, his stance, his gestures, his pauses and hesitations, may tell more about his real message than the words he is saying. By visual observation of his 'body language' you may learn how he *feels* about what he is saying, not just what he thinks." (The Royal Bank of Canada Monthly Newsletter, January 1979.)

When your husband is upset, and you are trying to listen reflectively, pay special attention to his "body language" for clues as to how he is feeling.

And I want to mention one very special form of nonverbal communication which is difficult to define in any specific terms, but which each of you have no doubt experienced. It is the sweet, silent communication between one spirit and another. This might be a communication from the Holy Ghost, or it may be a communication between two people whose spirits are in tune.

And after all your study and practice, when you still say the wrong thing at the wrong time in the wrong way, do not despair. Everyone makes mistakes. Repent, and try again. Do not give up, for it takes practice and experience.

Know what you mean, say what you mean. Try to understand your husband, what he is saying and how he is feeling, and learn to accept the feelings as well as the messages. Remember that to understand, you do not need to agree. "Let every man be swift to hear, slow to speak, slow to wrath: For the wrath of man worketh not the righteousness of God." (James 1:19-20.)

7

Housekeeper or Homemaker?

The excitement and festivities surrounding the wedding, gifts, and honeymoon probably kept you on the proverbial cloud for quite some time. By now perhaps you realize that being married is not just one prolonged date. You now have a home to look after.

That is a sobering realization.

As you look around your home and take stock of what needs to be done, the list is endless and staggering. There's the food to prepare, the house to clean, the laundry, ironing, and shopping to do. Then, add to that your husband and children with their needs, plus meetings to attend, callings to fill, family to visit, special days, nothing days—Help!

And what about that question of housekeeper or homemaker? Is there a difference?

Yes. A housekeeper is one who has charge of only the domestic tasks in a household. The tasks are an end in themselves for her. They are her priority.

A homemaker may also do all the necessary domestic tasks, but she is more concerned about the welfare of the people who live there, her family. The tasks are done to contribute to keeping her family comfortable, happy, and secure. The family is her priority.

Every one of you will be a unique homemaker. No two of you will do things exactly the same way, nor will you agree on what is most important for a happy home.

If you remember this, you won't be tempted to compare yourself to your mother-in-law, your super-tidy sister, or the Relief

Society president. Instead, work to find out what kind of home-maker you want to be, and then be it.

As a start, shut your eyes, relax, and think about the home you have always dreamed of having, not just the physical house and furnishings, but also the people and atmosphere. What do you see happening there? Family Home Evenings, basketball on the drive-way, Christmas celebrations, lots of friends, and maybe a budding drummer loosening the acoustic tiles off the rumpus room ceiling? Do you see daily family prayers and scripture studies? What do you see?

And what kind of mother fits into your picture? Is she a sweetly serene smiling woman helping a small pianist with his C major contrary scale, a blue-jean-clad gal rushing out with the kids for a fast game of 21 before supper, an elegantly dressed lady pre-siding in an immaculately appointed living room, or a woman scrubbing, waxing, polishing, scrubbing, waxing, polishing?

It's hard to know, isn't it? Kind of like seeing "through a glass, darkly" (see 1 Corinthians 13:12). But you need to think about it and set some goals, or you may end up being an unhappy home-maker, not at all measuring up to the kind you have the potential to become.

So, do think about it, and if you have some definite feelings about what kind of wife, mother and homemaker you want to be, write them down. Also note any particular features you want your home to have.

Regardless of your priorities as a homemaker, certain funda-mental principles will apply to you all. The first of these is *organi-zation.*

Have you ever heard or even said something like this: "One of these days I've just got to get organized, or at least find out what I'm not getting done. Maybe what I'm not doing isn't really worth doing or even worrying about. I've got to find out."

Unfortunately, the ability to organize is not an inborn trait. Fortunately, it is a skill that can be learned.

After ten years and six babies, one sister in our stake com-mented, "I not only didn't know how to organize before I married Bob; I didn't even know I was supposed to." Does that sound familiar to you?

By definition, organization is the process of putting together or arranging the parts into an orderly, functional whole. That is roughly equivalent to taking your grandmother's bag of accumulated yarn scraps, untangling the mess, rolling each color into a ball, and then crocheting them into uniform-sized granny squares. When you have artfully arranged these squares according to a chosen plan, and secured them into a warm and beautiful afghan, you have organized that bag of scraps.

To do a comparable thing to your many homemaking tasks you must

— want to get organized.
— identify all the elements that need to be organized.
— identify your priorities and goals.
— plan your work according to the priorities.
— set realistic goals, specific ones with deadlines.
— plan to accomplish the set goals.
— do it.

That's it. Over-simplified, for sure, but that's it. Now, let's look at each element and try to give you a step-by-step plan which will help you to become organized to the extent you wish.

Desire to Get Organized

No one can give you the desire to be organized. That must come from yourself.

Perhaps some Saturday night at ten o'clock when you are hurriedly washing clothes so your husband will have a clean shirt and socks for Church, vacuuming and dusting, and making an urgent attempt to prepare your Primary lesson, the thought slides through your frantic mind, "I've just got to get more organized. I don't want to live my whole life in a panic like this."

That is the time to make a firm commitment. Write it in your journal. Put it on the refrigerator. Stick it on the mirror in the bathroom.

Identify the Elements

Write down all the things you feel responsible for in your present situation, the elements that need to be organized. Consider the household duties, shopping, human relationships, letters, spirituality, assignments, and everything that is part of your concern. The list will astound you and boggle your mind. But put it all down. In a later step you will learn how to determine your priorities, and then you will be able to eliminate many things from this list.

Identify Your Priorities

You've heard about priorities all your life in the Church, but do you know how to determine what yours are?

Priorities are the things that are most important or urgent in a person's life. To be an effective person, you must find the way to accomplish those things which are priorities in your life and thereby fulfill what you see as the purpose of your life.

In identifying your priorities there are three categories of goals or objectives that you are to think of and record as fast as you can. You do not worry about practicality at this stage, only what you really want to do in each time frame.

Lifetime objectives. Set your oven timer for two minutes and write down all your lifetime dreams, ambitions, and objectives.

Next reset the timer for two more minutes and rethink your list —add to it, eliminate from it, or modify it in any way you see fit.

Your objectives for the next five years. Do the same for what you hope to accomplish in the next five years. Use two minutes to write and two minutes to revise.

If you had only six months left, what goals would you set? Again reset the timer and consider what you would choose to get done if you knew that you had six months to live. What would you spend those last six months doing? Use two minutes to write and two minutes to review.

This ends part one of the exercise. If your husband wanted to do it, too, it would be a great thing to discuss as you set family goals.

Look over your three lists and circle any item that is on all three lists. These are your priorities. Transfer them to this space by order of importance, number one being the most important.

1.   4.   7.

2.   5.   8.

3.   6.   9.

Any items that appeared twice are also high priorities. Continue your list here.

10.	13.	16.
11.	14.	17.
12.	15.	18.

That was fairly simple, wasn't it? As your family situation changes, you may want to repeat the exercise.

While achievement of goals is important, the development of your personality and character are equally important. To reach into this area, I am reminded of a concept I heard presented at a youth conference: "Pretend that you died and this is your funeral. What would you like someone to say about you in the eulogy?"

The girls giggled a little, then they started to respond with things like, "I'd like her to say I was kind, compassionate, cheerful, honest, a good person, a faithful friend, and a dedicated mother."

The girls were then told that if they wanted to be like that in forty or fifty years, they should start working at it now, with real intent. That is good counsel. What kind of person do you want to become? What kind of person do you want to be remembered as?

Add these characteristics to your priority lists. Actual written goals and objectives are important. "It has been well said that a goal not written down generally turns out to be only a wish." (Ernest Eberhard, Jr., "How to Help Nonmembers in Your Own Family," *Ensign,* October 1977, page 64.)

In the years I have worked with women and girls, I have never met one who deliberately chose to be a disorganized, slovenly, miserable woman, always behind in her work, late for her meetings, and upset with her husband and children. Why then do so many women end up that way?

Perhaps they did never decide *not* to end up that way. Perhaps they didn't know how to end up happy and effective. My purpose is to teach you how.

Plan Your Work According to Your Priorities

There are several key steps between identifying your priority and actually putting it into action. Many know what they want and should do but never seem to quite make it happen.

This step in getting organized is crucial. Review your list of elements that need to be organized into your overall homemaking. Compare it to your priority lists. Beside every task that will help achieve priority number one, put a number one; then beside all the tasks that relate to number two priority, put a number two, and so on for as many priorities as you have chosen.

At the end of this step any tasks which do not fit under one of your priorities need to be closely scrutinized. Ask yourself, "Why do I feel I need to do this job?" If you can't think of a good reason, draw a bold line through it and never think of it again. If a task does not contribute to your priorities, get rid of it.

This step is no good unless you really erase those tasks from your mind and quit letting them worry you and make you feel like you're less of a homemaker than you ought to be.'

Just to be sure you understand what to do to complete this step; if your priority number four is to have an orderly and efficient household, then all the tasks on your list from step two which would help to achieve an orderly and efficient household should have the number four beside them.

You have the idea? And you have done the correlation? Now, let's go on to the next step.

Set Realistic Goals

You, like me, have probably set some grand goals in your time. Do these goals sound familiar: I want to be a better person; I want to get organized; I'd like to be more spiritual. But setting such lofty goals does not always produce results. Why? Because they are too general. Goals need to be *specific*. Add to that the concept that to get any action you must set specific goals with specific deadlines, and you are on the way to changing your life.

For example, the goal of becoming more spiritual is so vague and nebulous, so general, that it's difficult to measure progress. And when there is no deadline or time limit, I never feel an urgency to do anything.

As I followed the counsel to be specific, my goal became this: I will become a more spiritual person by reading the scriptures for fifteen minutes every morning, never missing my personal morning and nightly prayers, and studying the Sunday School and Relief Society lessons before going to classes each week.

Do you see any difference? Now at the end of each day I know whether or not I have accomplished my goals of scripture reading and prayers. Every Sunday I know whether or not I have read my lessons. The deadlines were built in.

The keys to setting realistic goals are to

—identify your priorities.
—set specific, related goals.
—set definite deadlines for each goal.
—be realistic.
—follow through and do it.
—evaluate your progress.

The test of a specific goal is: Will I know when I have done it and when I have not?

Suppose one of your goals from the previous steps is to cook better meals. Yet that is not a specific goal. You must build in the specific things you will do to make the meals you prepare better. For example, you might decide to serve two vegetables with each dinner and include some form of fruit in every breakfast. You will know for sure whether you have done these things or not.

Look at your top five priorities. Practice stating them as specific goals. I cannot leave you sufficient room in this book for you to state your goals, but let me ease you into the next step and the plan book.

Get a book or three-ringed binder to use as your plan book. In the front of this book list your priorities. Then write each priority as a specific goal and set some reasonable deadlines.

Plan to Accomplish the Set Goals

Working to accomplish the set goals takes the goal out of the thinking stage and gets it into the doing stage. Your plan book can be almost as good as a personal secretary. Record what needs to be done and when it needs to be done. That way you do not have to keep worrying about details.

My plan book contains the following:

—A list of my priorities.

—Goals for the year; I usually write these at the beginning of the year.

—Monthly goals; I slot the year's goals into the month they best fit into. Some are obvious (birthdays, seasonal celebrations, gardening). At the beginning of each new month, I modify the plan for that month, depending on specific needs.

—Weekly goals; every Monday morning I plot what must be done before Friday. This is determined by the monthly goals plus routine tasks.

—Daily plan; this I do each morning. This reminds you to do your scripture reading, write in your journal, talk to your husband about Jeremy's recital, do a dark load of wash, shorten your husband's new trousers.

That's it. That's what a plan book contains. Now, before you throw up your hands and say it's too rigid, too structured, consider that you are the person who makes the lists. You can put as much or as little into a day as you wish. Plus, you always know that the unexpected can happen and ruin your plan. You just must be prepared to be flexible if the need arises, but for the great majority of days you will get much more accomplished with a plan than you will without one. That is why I recommend a book which will lay open by itself. Every time you walk by it, it needs to be there to remind you of what else needs to be done today. When I do not plan my days, like during holidays, I sometimes go the whole day forgetting to even write in my journal. It is so easy to get caught up in activities and totally forget priority things.

To be an effective homemaker, you must get done those things which you feel are important to you and your family. A plan can help you to do that.

Doing it is the final, crucial step. No amount of marvelous planning will make one shred of difference if you don't do what you've planned.

Many women are hampered when it comes to doing housework because they either feel there is so much to do they don't know where to start, or that they can leave chores for later because they have the whole day, or that they just would rather do things other than work. You are your own supervisor. You have to be self-motivated and sufficiently disciplined to go ahead on your own and do what needs to be done, whether you feel like it or not.

Being motivated can help you work wonders. Think how much you can get done if you want to go to a movie in half an hour, or if you have company coming for dinner—that's motivation. An itemized plan can do the same thing.

Watch to see when you are most energetic, when you get the most done in the shortest time. Be it morning, noon, or night, that is your prime time. When you have challenging tasks to do, you should schedule them during the prime hours.

Daryl Hoole, author of *The Art of Homemaking,* introduced her now-famous "work smarter not harder" concept. Use your head as well as your elbows, and maybe you'll be able to end up using your elbows less. Have your husband look over your responsibilities, and ask his opinion on how you might become more efficient. With his fresh perspective he may have some good ideas for streamlining your jobs. My husband has simplified many of my procedures.

A homemaker's work often gets boring because it is so repetitive, and it seems hopeless because it self-destructs every twenty-four hours. But until someone invents a self-refilling lasagna or a bed that makes itself, there is little else to do except to make the best of it.

Here are some rules of thumb to help make your tasks easier:
—Establish a daily routine for the jobs that must be done, like beds, dishes, laundry, etc. Why waste time trying to decide whether to do them now or later? Just do them.
—Let each person help with the work; train small children to make beds, put dirty clothes in the laundry, help with dishes, etc.
—Never leave the kitchen after a meal until the dishes are done.
—Fold laundry as soon as it is dry to save ironing. Put clothes away as soon as they are folded.
—Set the oven timer for ten minutes just before you go to bed and pick up in the living room.
—Set the breakfast table at night.

—Get up early enough to comb your hair and put on some-thing quick but attractive; nightie, slippers, and curlers worn until noon are guaranteed to cut your efficiency by half.

—Do the basic necessary tasks early in the day before starting on a project or hobby.

—Do at least one heavy or unpleasant chore each day so they aren't all piled up on Saturday.

—Keep the clutter under control by throwing or putting things away.

—Keep duplicate cleaning supplies where they are used often.

—Do not start too many jobs at once; you may run out of energy before you're done and end up with major messes in four places.

—Keep the next four months of calendar pages posted some-where near the kitchen phone. Maintain this as the official master family calendar.

—Put things away after use; have you ever stopped to add up the time you spend looking for things?

—Get tasks done before they become a crisis; no clean ironed shirt for husband on Sunday morning is a crisis.

—Maintain your house each day so it doesn't require a major clean-up each Saturday; and try to remember that a clean house is not necessarily antiseptic.

—Do not spend more time on a task than it is worth.

One day when the washing machine breaks down, the toilet gets plugged, your two-year-old spills red food coloring *all* over, you forget to add salt to the bread, you lift out the back of a good polyester shirt with a too-hot iron, and you are worried about the outdated food you are afraid to use for fear of food poisoning but which you dare not throw out because it would be wasteful, call your mother and tell her thanks for all she did for you when you lived at home. And tell her you love her. Then, if you feel so in-clined, cry.

No matter how well you plan, how pure your intentions, or how diligently you work, you will still have some dreadful days. So do we all—life is like that.

Since life is unpredictable, don't get rigid about your plan. If something comes up, or your husband gets an unexpected day off, know when to set the plan aside. Don't let the things that matter least take precedence over the things that matter the most. People are always more important than things. The house and laundry will wait.

This is as far as I'm going on this homemaker theme. You are on your own now. Read, watch, listen to the sisters around you, and learn all you can. Slowly you will discover what kind of homemaker you are becoming.

And don't let anyone tell you that staying at home and being a wife, mother and homemaker makes you unimportant or a failure just because you don't earn a salary. Of all the professional jobs I've ever had, this one is undoubtedly the hardest and the most rewarding.

Enjoy doing your own work. In a few years you will have small people you need to teach by letting them do, and for the next fifteen years you will have to let them share the work. Do you know that it could be twenty years before you can do all your work alone again? So, enjoy it, or at least endure it gracefully.

8

Money Matters

"Money may not be the most important thing in the world, but it certainly comes a close second to whatever is" — so some folks say.

I don't believe that money is the second most important thing in the world, but I do recognize that money or the lack of it will have a tremendous impact on your life.

I also recognize that your particular financial status may range anywhere from great to decidedly dismal right down to definitely desperate.

Regardless of where you fit on such a scale, certain money facts are the same. Money in and of itself has no value. Like the alphabet, it takes on meaning and value only when it is used. It can be used to uplift and make happy, or to downgrade and destroy. In today's industrialized societies of interdependence, money is necessary to procure food, clothing, and shelter. Each cash dollar can only be spent once. You are not the bank or the government.

Along with these general money facts, there are further specifics about you and your husband's money that you need to know.

Do you know how much money you really have each month? Does your combined salary represent how much you have to spend? Salary generally represents the gross amount you are offered for doing a job. No one actually receives that amount, however, because of income tax, insurance, and pension deductions.

What is left after deductions is called net salary. Is this the amount of money you really have? Yes and no.

The net salary is what comes into your home. But before you are free to spend it on a rug, a stereo, or a trip to Mexico, you must first pay your fixed expenses, such as tithes and offerings, savings for various specifics, rent or mortgage payments, utilities, other insurances, and loan payments.

Is what is left after these are paid yours to spend as you wish? Again, the answer is yes and no.

There are other expenses which, while flexible, are essential to maintain your life—food and clothing.

Are you getting discouraged? It's no wonder, but this is the end of the line. Whatever money is left now is yours to spend as the two of you choose. This bit that is left is what I call "choice income" because you really do have a choice in how it is spent.

Gross income minus the total of regular payroll deductions minus fixed expenses minus essential living expenses equals "choice income."

Often it is also harsh for young couples starting out because there is usually little left as "choice income." And, because it is so harsh, many will not accept it. This refusal to accept the facts of monetary life can create some severe conditions in a marriage.

A woman who does not understand the difference between gross and choice income may get really frustrated and wonder: "What's happening to all that money? Why won't he let me spend more of it? Did I marry a miser?"

If both partners lack understanding about the realities of money management, they may go on a giant spending spree each payday, only to be faced with an irate landlord, discontinued utilities, insufficient food to last until the next payday, guilt over nonpayment of tithes, and a deteriorating life-style that belies their net income.

Credit cards are almost as readily available as bubble gum cards in North America where buying on credit is firmly entrenched into the life-style. Many couples get hopelessly in debt because it is so easy.

Elder Marvin J. Ashton said, "The American Bar Association

recently indicated that 89 percent of all divorces could be traced to quarrels and accusations over money." (Marvin J. Ashton, *One for the Money*, Deseret Book Co., 1975, page 8.)

Money is a touchy topic and some couples never discuss it except when they fight about it.

The following three steps may help you to avoid these serious consequences of poor money management.

First, because two people are involved, even if only one earns the money, there must be an open discussion about finances. You need to learn how each of you feels about money, how much will be coming in every month, if the money will go into a joint account, if there will be any personal allowances, what the money should be used for, who will keep the books, if any credit will be used, what the valid reasons for debt might be, if you will use cash or checks, and how to develop a budget.

Second, recognizing that almost everything costs either time, effort, or money, both of you must have a desire to manage all your resources wisely. Without the desire and commitment to the concept of wise use of resources, including money, nothing can be done.

The third step is to accept a specific system or budget. Decide which of you will serve as the family accountant. Then get a simple account book and outline your basic monetary system, or budget, which you both agree to follow in the dispersing of your mutual funds.

Faithfully and systematically record each month's expected expenses; as each month rolls around, record what was actually spent in each major category. *Keep* all significant receipts, expense records, and other data needed to file your income tax. (And you might want to either keep all cancelled checks for major purchases or make a permanent record of them. This is useful for checking back on the cost and life of a particular appliance, for example.)

Outlined here is the skeleton of the system which my husband and I have used for many years, from the lean years of college until the present. Fill in the blanks with your own particulars and see if it helps to identify the possible division of your money for a month:

Financial System (budget) *of* _____

Expected gross annual income: _____
Expected gross monthly income _____
Expected net monthly income _____

Expenses:
Tithes and offerings _____
Savings _____
Rent or mortgage _____
Utilities _____
Insurance _____
Loan payments _____
Personal allowances _____
Total fixed expenses _____

Flexible expenses:
Food _____
Clothing _____
Educational _____
Recreational _____
Seasonal _____
Other _____
Total flexible expenses _____
Grand total of expenses _____ _____ _____
Balance or choice income _____

This system is based on a "them" and "us" theory. "Them" must be paid before "us" can spend money on whatever we want. "Them" represents all necessary costs, fixed and flexible.

If your total expenses are even a dollar less than your net income, you are living within your means. Basically, that is what money management is all about.

Certainly you could now get into discussions about what kinds of things are most important, from a value point of view, in spending that precious choice income. That is up to you. Just be sure you learn to manage so you have some choice income left.

Probably one good characteristic to develop in the material-
istic society we live in is *buyer resistance,* a willingness to wait or
even do without. Money management is quite like time management. You know what you want; don't let some advertising copy
writer decide for you. Get from your money what you think you
should.

The rest of this chapter is a collection of relevant material that
could help you to stay or become financially stable.

Establish a realistic and personalized life-style. Do not get
caught up in the "keeping up with the Joneses or the Hinckle-
himers" syndrome. Be a unique couple. Choose your own priorities and goals, then spend your money to achieve them. Recently I
visited a single girl in our ward. She has a comfortable though not
elegant apartment. She explained, "My priority is travel, not furniture." I was impressed with her wisdom.

Write your anticipated *actual* expenses in dollars into the
month's budget plan. You can then see how it affects the overall
picture. It is easy to eliminate foolish expenditures before they
occur. Pencil is easy to erase.

Savings should become a priority habit, a fixed expense. "Take
it off the top or you'll never have any savings" is a true statement.
If you plan to save whatever is left over at the end of the month,
you will not accumulate much. Church leaders recommend you
have an emergency savings fund available as part of your year's
supply. Save for a definite purpose, and shop around for the best
interest. Check not only the rate but also how it is calculated and
how often.

Personal allowances, however small, can provide an area of
complete privacy in your marriage. This money can be spent
foolishly, hoarded, or used in whatever way you wish. It's a great
thing, even if it's only twenty dollars.

Credit, like money, is not good or bad. It can be either, depending on how you use it. It is wise to establish a credit rating by
purchasing something on credit and paying it off as specified.
Then, should you ever need to borrow money, the bank will have
access to a record that rates you as a good risk. Be aware, however, that too many credit cards, or the unrestrained use of one,
can sink you fast. I would suggest that you never charge groceries

or luxuries. Establish a maximum ceiling per month and pay off the total balance at the end of each month. Then you can have the convenience of credit without the added costs and headaches. If you should lose your card, immediately notify the issuing company.

"Let us avoid debt. . . . Let us straightly and strictly live within our incomes and save a little," is counsel given by President J. Reuben Clark. It is still excellent advice. We've been counseled to avoid debt, except for basic long-range investments, such as buying a home or investing in advanced schooling. If you must borrow, shop around for the lowest interest rate you are eligible for.

In today's high inflation economy, the answer may not be to try to earn more dollars, but rather to get greater value from each dollar you presently have. Develop as many skills as possible so you can be self-reliant and save service costs in sewing, painting, decorating, plumbing, etc.

The Lord explains his basic economic system:

> Will a man rob God? Yet ye have robbed me. But ye say: Wherein have we robbed thee? In tithes and offerings.
>
> Bring ye all the tithes into the storehouse, that there may be meat in mine house, and prove me now herewith, saith the Lord of hosts, if I will not open you the windows of heaven, and pour you out a blessing, that there shall not be room enough to receive it.
>
> And I will rebuke the devourer for your sakes, and he shall not destroy the fruits of your ground; neither shall your vine cast her fruit before the time in the field, saith the Lord of hosts.
>
> And all nations shall call you blessed: for ye shall be a delightsome land, saith the Lord of hosts. (Malachi 3:8, 10-12.)

That is an all-encompassing promise of blessings for those who obey the Lord's economic law. I wouldn't consider disregarding it. I can't afford to disregard it.

I know none of you needs a lesson on how to spend money, but I have included a few buying tips that might help you to spend more prudently:

Buy to satisfy a need. If you don't need it, don't buy it.

Cultivate buyer resistance: be suspect of advertising.

A bargain is not a bargain unless you need the item and would have bought it at a higher price.

Wait for two or three days before closing the deal on any major purchase.

Browse around as a Friday night outing now and again. Carry a booklet in which you note the prices of things you buy regularly and are planning to buy.

Do not buy top-line merchandise unless the extra money will appreciably improve your standard of living.

Recognize that most stores are set up so the highest priced produce is at eye level. If you want to save money you will have to adopt the stoop and reach system.

If your family won't eat it, don't buy it.

Shop regularly and completely when you get groceries to avoid midweek trips which cost time and money.

Check out thrift shops, flea markets, and garage sales.

Check out factory outlets, clearance centers, and discount houses. Along with the unusable stuff you will find items with only minor flaws.

When buying clothes, read the care label. A pastel item that must be dry cleaned will be expensive to maintain.

Use the catalogue to order standard items. This saves gas, parking, time and being jostled in a crowded store.

Save all cash receipt slips for clothing and other items that may need to be returned.

Submit the necessary papers to validate warranties and guarantees by the prescribed time; keep service manuals.

Buy food in season; clothes, cars, and sports equipment out of season.

Be mindful of consumer aid information available in your area, and use it.

Money is only temporal, but its effects can have eternal consequences. Learn all you can, for after all is said and speculated upon, you and your husband are totally responsible for the financial affairs and the overall welfare of your family unit.

The key to whether you are happy or miserable with your particular circumstances depends almost entirely upon your attitude. "Sufficient for our needs" is a good philosophy that will allow you to be happy, though sometimes poor.

On the other hand, if you get all your satisfaction from material things, no amount of money will ever be enough to satisfy you completely.

These five principles of economic constancy, outlined by President N. Eldon Tanner in the October 1979 General Conference, are a good summary of this chapter:

1. Pay an honest tithing.
2. Live on less than you earn.
3. Learn to distinguish between needs and wants.
4. Develop and live within a budget.
5. Be honest in all your financial affairs.

"But before ye seek for riches, seek ye for the kingdom of God. And after ye have obtained a hope in Christ ye shall obtain riches, if ye seek them; and ye will seek them for the intent to do good — to clothe the naked, and to feed the hungry, and to liberate the captive, and to administer relief to the sick and the afflicted." (Jacob 2:18-19.)

9

Food

"Man shall not live by bread alone." But he cannot live without it, either. Besides, he enjoys it so much, especially when it is tasty and served on time.

Food preparation is generally accepted as part of a home-maker's responsibilities. This plus its regular recurrence, regardless of rain, snow, exams, or nausea, makes it a major challenge for most girls.

Some of you will love your kitchen, the heart of your home. Others of you will strongly dislike your kitchen, regarding it more as a battlefield where it is a solid three-pound block of hamburger against you and your half-hour deadline. For you, just looking at the beautiful, full-colored illustrations in magazines and cook-books gives you heartburn.

Nevertheless, food preparation is essential to the happy home. And while this chapter is not intended to make you into an ac-complished gourmet cook, it is designed to keep you alive in your kitchen.

Perhaps you have believed that food preparation is just cooking, and now as you have had some problems with it, you feel incompetent. After all, any fool should be able to cook, shouldn't she?

Well, actually, food preparation is much more involved than just cooking. In fact, there are six, distinct steps: planning, shopping, storage, cooking, serving, and cleaning up.

That's why you are having trouble. You aren't incompetent. Food preparation is a complicated, time-consuming, difficult process which is fraught with many kinds of culinary disasters. Only in the kitchen will you encounter a baked potato which explodes in the oven, five carefully saved containers of left-overs with fur growing on them in your refrigerator, or pastry so hard your father-in-law's piece of pie flies off his dish when he attempts to cut through the pie with his fork.

There is no doubt about it, the kitchen can be a rough place. Once you learn some of the skills needed to properly prepare food, it gets easier. Here is a step-by-step plan to make you more competent in your kitchen:

Planning

Some of you grew up with mothers who planned detailed daily menus; others of you had moms who planned only dinner menus for a week at a time; and others of you have never seen a menu except in a restaurant. No matter, for how you plan is not important. But it is important to plan so you will know what groceries to buy to keep your family healthy.

There are only two main reasons why you have to eat at all: a) food provides necessary nutrients and energy for your body, and b) food provides comfort and enjoyment.

To meet the first consideration, simply follow the food guide. The amounts of food from each group that are required each day vary with a person's age, sex, and kind of work. So, suffice it to say that you should include foods from each group each day.

Basic Food Groups

Protein — meat, fish, poultry, eggs, cheese
Cereals — whole grain and other breads and cereals
Fruit — citrus and other
Vegetables — leafy green, yellow, and other
Milk — milk and milk products

To meet the second consideration, choose foods from each group which are acceptable to you both. Discuss this with him at dinner tonight. By the end of the meal you should know what foods you both like and enjoy, what foods you dislike but will eat, and what foods you detest and would rather starve than eat.

Once you know this you will at least know what not to include in your plans.

Then you will want to make each meal as enjoyable as possible. Start by having you consider how you would like a sandwich made of two slices of white bread with a soda cracker filling. It would ward off starvation, but would you like it? Would it give you comfort and enjoyment?

Think of the classic ham and lettuce sandwich. Of the two, which would you prefer? Are you getting an idea of how to plan for enjoyment?

Try this dinner menu: scrambled eggs, mashed potatoes, creamed cauliflower, vanilla pudding. This meal has nutritional value, it is true. It has protein (eggs), two vegetables (potatoes and cauliflower), and a milk-based dessert. Sounds awful, though, doesn't it? Why?

Everything is bland in flavor, soft in texture, and more or less the same colorless color. How could you improve it? (Throwing it out is not one of the options.)

You could keep the eggs and garnish them with paprika to add color and flavor. Substitute garlic bread for the potatoes. This is still white, but you have added flavor and crispness in the crust. Then, in place of the cauliflower, serve a tray of raw tomato wedges, carrot and celery sticks, and a few pickles. You have now introduced color, flavor, and crunch. Finally, you could keep the dessert and serve it with either a crisp cookie or some fruit topping.

Are you getting the idea? Here are the rules for planning pleasing meals: choose foods from each group each day; choose the foods which both of you enjoy or are willing to try; plan for *variety* of flavor, color, textures, and even temperatures; and be flexible and creative; have fun with your meals.

Take a few minutes now and plan a dinner. Write down your sample menu. Then check it against the rules and see how you did.

Shopping

Once you've chosen the foods to eat, the next step is to get them. You can shop at specialty shops like the butcher, the baker, and the green grocer; or you can shop at a supermarket near your home. One method is not any better than the other. It is strictly a matter of individual preferences.

Once you've chosen your store, figure out the best time to shop and then learn the floor plan.

Next, check your plans against the supplies you have on hand and make your list. You will save shopping time and lessen the chance of forgetting some things if you list your needs according to the layout of the store.

Study the weekly grocery specials. Some girls plan their menus around the specials. We have eaten according to what was on sale for years.

Finally, check to see how much money is budgeted for food this week, eat before going shopping, take your list, and shop with cash instead of an open-ended check.

Once in the store, buy everything on your list so you won't have to make extra trips during the week. A small calculator is handy for keeping a running total. If you exceed your limit, you can decide what to return to the shelves before you get to the cashier.

Do not buy on impulse. Be wary of gimmicks and dramatic displays. Use the stoop and reach system to find lower priced shelf goods. Buy staples when they are on sale to build up your year's supply. And watch the expiration date on perishables.

Fresh fruits and vegetables, ideally, are firm, crisp, and blemish-free. Reduced price produce can be a good buy: over-ripe tomatoes are good stewed or in chili and spaghetti sauce; over-ripe bananas make delicious banana bread; soft apples are great for pies and other desserts; and citrus fruit is often still juicy on the inside while getting a little peaked on the outside.

Unit pricing is helpful when comparing the prices of various sizes of similar products. But, when buying meat, rather than price per pound, price per serving will be a more accurate comparison as it accounts for waste and shrinkage. Boneless roasts will serve about three to four per pound; bone-in roasts will feed two or three per pound; whole birds serve about two per pound; steaks serve two or three per pound; and ground meat serves about three per pound.

Know the cuts.

1. Round
2. Sirloin Tip
3. Rump
4. Sirloin
5. Porterhouse
6. T-Bone
7. Wing
8. Tenderloin
9. Rib
10. Short Ribs
11. Blade
12. Chuck
13. Cross-rib or
    Chuck Short Rib
14. Shoulder
15. Neck
16. Brisket
17. Plate
18. Flank
19. Shank

Most tender

Medium tender

Less tender

Cook correctly to achieve maximum flavor and tenderness

Roast, broil, fry or barbecue

May roast, broil or fry, but for extra tenderness braise or pot roast

Braise, pot roast or stew (numbers 10 through 18 are often an excellent buy)

I will outline these methods of cooking meats a little later in this chapter.

I have included the above diagram so you can see at a glance what the beef cuts are. Since meat is the most expensive item on your list, it would be well to acquaint yourself with this chart and to learn what the different cuts are like.

Filet mignon, the tenderloin of beef, is considered to be the most flavored of all beef cuts. But lesser cuts like chuck are as nutritious and as flavorful at a much lower price. You need to know how to cook them to make them tender and juicy. In fact, I was interested to read the following: "Lesser beef cuts can be used successfully in braising with excellent results. I particularly like to use the *rump pot roast,* the *brisket,* and the *chuck pot roast.* More expensive cuts such as *eye round* and *sirloin tip* are usually dry and less flavorful." (Perla Meyers, *From Market to Kitchen Cookbook,* Harper & Row, 1979, page 3.)

For more information call your local branch of your state's department of agriculture. Request their pamphlets about the meats available in your area. This is generally a free service. (While you are talking to them, ask them to send you their list of publications. You will find much helpful information is available for the asking.)

Storing

Without adequate storage, food will deteriorate and be neither nutritious nor tasty.

Light, temperature, and moisture are the factors which most affect the keeping qualities of food. In general, keep food cool, dark, and moist for meats, baked goods; keep fruits and vegetables dry.

Fresh meat will keep only about three days in your refrigerator. If you plan to keep it longer, wrap it well, label it, and freeze it.

Freezer storage time varies with the kind of meat, but at 0°F. or -18° C. beef will keep about a year; pork is good for four months; whole poultry keeps about a year; and cut-up poultry will keep about a half a year. Ground meat keeps about two or three months. Fatty meats and cut up meats have a shorter keeping time.

Freezer burn is caused by drying, and it results in discoloration, loss of texture, and flavor. It is not harmful.

Can food that has thawed be refrozen? If the food is still very cold, it can be refrozen. If the food is starting to get warm, then either use it right away or cook it, then freeze it.

Hot food and cold food do not spoil as readily as does warm food. Always remember that the cold freezer air is extremely dry air. Wrap meats, vegetables, fruit, or baked goods air tight when you put them in or they will get dry and hard.

Most fruits and vegetables come home in a plastic bag, which is fine for short-term storage. But after several days, moisture collects and the produce will start to rot.

Root vegetables have a much longer holding life, but they will rot, sprout, or go spongy if they are left where it is warm. They need cold air circulating around them.

Dry items like flour, cereal, and milk powder should be kept dry and cool. Nothing keeps indefinitely, so date the things and use them within a year.

Cooking

Cooking is intended to improve the food, to make it more tender, flavorful, palatable, and attractive. Over-cooking or burning does none of these things.

Many foods are already tender, flavorful, palatable, and attractive in their natural state. Use these raw whenever you can. In addition to the traditional salad vegetables, nearly all vegetables are tasty uncooked. Only the high starch vegetables, such as corn and potatoes, are not suitable because they are too hard to digest raw.

There are two common methods of cooking vegetables. Do not overcook.

To boil vegetables use the least amount of water possible and cook them in the shortest time for best color, flavor, and food value. Put prepared vegetables into a saucepan, add about one-half cup water, sprinkle with salt, cover, bring to a boil over high heat, then *reduce* heat to medium or medium low. Cook only until vegetables are tender.

To bake vegetables put the prepared vegetables in a greased baking dish, sprinkle with salt, dot with butter or margarine, cover, and bake in an oven along with a roast or casserole. Cook until tender. Serve right in the baking dish. Potatoes need their skins pierced for baking. Even a small potato makes a big mess if it explodes in the oven.

Meat cookery is important, too. If you do not use proper methods, you can turn even the nicest meat into dry, tasteless leather. The following are recommended cooking methods for beef.

Roast. This is best for large tender roasts. Place the seasoned meat, fat side up, in an uncovered pan. Do *not* add water. Cook at 325°. (Rare—approximately twenty minutes per pound or an internal temperature of 140°; medium—approximately thirty minutes per pound or an internal temperature of 160°; well done —approximately thirty-five minutes per pound or an internal temperature of 170°.)

Broil. This is best for tender steaks and other thin cuts. Slash the fat edge to prevent curling, then place meat on a cold broiler pan and broil four to five inches from the heat. Season after browning. Broil about seven minutes per side for a ¾-inch steak done medium well.

Pot roast. This is best for less tender small roasts. Brown the meat on all sides. Add one cup of liquid, season the meat, cover and simmer slowly on stove top or in the oven. Add more liquid if necessary. You may add vegetables during the last forty-five minutes.

Braise. This is best for less tender roasts. Place seasoned meat fat side up in a pan. Add about an inch of water, cover, and cook in a 325° oven. Add more liquid if it is required.

For thin cuts brown the meat on both sides in a small amount of fat. Then add one cup of liquid, cover, and simmer on the top of the stove until tender.

For those of you who want to know how to prepare the traditional Christmas turkey, here are step-by-step instructions.

To thaw the turkey keep the original wrapper intact. Set the bird in a pan and let it sit in the refrigerator for two or three days, depending on the size; or put it in a double brown bag and set it in your basement for twenty-four hours. If you are in a hurry, put the bird in a sink of cold water for about eight hours or until you can remove the giblets. Once the turkey is thawed, remove the giblets and neck from the cavity and rinse it out.

Stuff the turkey just moments before you put the bird in the oven. Use your favorite recipe, season it well. Fill both cavities with stuffing, using skewers to close the skin flaps. Tuck the legs under the skin band. Then rub butter, margarine, or drippings on the sides and bottom of the pan and all over the bird.

Use the lowest rack in an oven set at 325° to roast your turkey. Put the turkey on its back in the pan, cover it with foil to prevent the breast meat from drying out. Cook it covered until about the final hour.

During the last hour, baste the bird about four or five times. Turn the heat up to 400° to brown the skin. Watch it closely, and when it is golden turn the heat back down to 325°.

Do not overcook the turkey. It is done when the thigh moves easily or when the internal temperature reaches 185°. If you use a meat thermometer, stick it in the breast so it will not touch any bone.

Approximate Cooking Time Guide — 325° Oven

Weight	*Cooking Time*
6 - 8 pounds	3½ hours
8 - 12 pounds	4½ hours
12 - 16 pounds	5½ hours
16 - 20 pounds	6½ hours
20 - 24 pounds	7 hours

Once you determine that the bird is done, remove it from the oven. Let it set for thirty minutes with the lid *off*. Then remove it to a tray or platter. Take the stuffing out immediately.

If you will serve immediately keep the stuffing hot and have the turkey carved while you make the gravy. If you aren't serving for several hours, spread the stuffing on a cookie sheet or large bowl and set it in a cold room. Also set the turkey in to chill. Then, just before dinner, carve the turkey, arrange it on a tray, cover it, and put it in a 250° oven to heat. Heat as much stuffing as you will use, and keep the rest in the refrigerator. We routinely cook our turkeys from midnight until early morning. Then we have the oven free for other meal preparations. I'm never pressed just before dinner because the turkey is all carved, the stuffing set, and everything is ready.

I prepare gravy just before we serve. Put the roaster with the drippings on a medium high burner and brown all the meat drippings. When there is only fat loose in the pan, drain it off. Add a generous amount of water and return it to the stove. Let it boil gently and stir it often to dissolve all the browned-on meat juices.

If you need only a little gravy, remove some of this liquid to save for fresh gravy another day. It freezes beautifully.

For now, remove the pan from the heat and add a mixture of flour and water which you have shaken to make sure there are no lumps. Stir it in well, then return the pan to the stove. Stir constantly and bring it to a boil. Season it well with plenty of salt. You should have smooth, rich, delicious brown gravy.

Enjoy your holiday dinner. When you do it in stages, it is actually very simple to prepare a turkey.

The following is a collection of cooking tips:

Keep at least one sharp knife in your kitchen to save time, frustration, and smashed tomatoes.

To slice meat for beef Stroganoff or sukiyaki, first freeze the meat for about an hour until it is firm.

Keep some grated Parmesan cheese, a can of paprika, and some fresh or dried parsley on hand for quick garnishes.

Buy large quantities of hamburger when it is on sale, brown it, drain it, and freeze it in meal-sized quantities. Then it is ready to use in casseroles, spaghetti sauce, etc.

When baking juicy pies, put a teflon cookie sheet or a piece of foil on the lower rack to catch the drippings.

If you are making pizza, casserole, cake or pie, make a double batch and freeze one for some busy day down the way.

Keep the oven rack in the center unless your recipe specifies otherwise.

Never underestimate how long it will take to make up a new recipe.

Stick to tried-and-true recipes when entertaining. Do your experimenting on your own time.

When you turn on your oven for part of a meal, see if the rest of the cooking can be done in there as well. It will save stove top watching and energy. You can cook nearly anything in the oven from scrambled eggs to rice.

Do not leave your kitchen when the burner is on high unless you set the oven timer to remind you when to turn it down. If you don't, you could return to burned potatoes, melting pots, or worse, fat that has ignited and set your kitchen on fire.

Soaking vegetables in water will keep them crisp, but it also dissolves the many water-soluble nutrients. If you soak vegetables for Sunday, cook them in that water or use it in the gravy.

Remember that metal utensils will scratch off the teflon coating on pans.

Check with your mother-in-law for the recipes of your husband's favorites.

To cook nonsticky, fluffy rice use regular pearl or long grain rice. Wash it several times until the water is quite clear. Use a heavy saucepan that has a tight fitting lid. Add an equal amount of water and rice, or use the Chinese cook's trick (measure the water level above the rice with your index finger; it should come to just above the first knuckle). Heat over high heat until it starts to boil, then reduce heat to medium and set the timer for ten minutes. At the end of the time turn off the heat. *Do not remove lid* for at least ten minutes.

I know you've heard about foolproof pastries, and you've managed to make all of them hard. My children mix this one up for us. When they were tiny, I would give them some dough which they would play with until it was gray. Then they would bake it. It was still tender. This makes enough for at least three double-crust pies and will keep covered in the fridge for about two weeks. After that it turns blue and fuzzy.

1 cup pastry lard   3 cups flour
¼ cup margarine   ½ cup cold water
1 tsp. salt

Combine the *softened* lard and margarine. Stir in the salt. Add flour, 1 cup at a time, mixing well each time. Add water. At first it will not combine. Keep working it. I use my hands. Then it will get very sticky, and finally it will absorb all the liquid and get smooth. You will need to roll it with a fairly generous amount of flour. It will roll very thin; it is pliable and easy to use.

To make tasty homemade soup, the important thing is preparing the stock. Boil the bones slowly in lots of water for several hours. Remove the bones and chill the stock. I put it in the refrigerator overnight. The fat will solidify and is easily removed. Season it well with bouillon cubes, salt, etc. Make only as much soup as you can use in two days. The stock can be frozen for fresh soup later.

Learning to cook is a gradual process. Maintain an attitude of adventure, a willingness to try new things combined with patience and perseverance. Keep track of ideas that work for you. You will soon develop your own cooking style. Eat your mistakes and keep trying to improve. You will.

Serving the Food

There are many ways to serve a meal. I am going to stick to the simple, family style service where the food is placed on the table and everyone passes it around. If you are interested in formal service, check out a hostess book from your library.

The main task here is to get all the food on the table at the appointed time in the condition it should be in—hot food hot and cold food cold.

Have your table set early. Later you can teach your children to do this for you. A prepared table is very reassuring, both to you and to your husband. Even if the meal is a bit late, when your husband sees the table set he knows you are working at it.

Set the table so it looks nice, even for a simple meal. It is another way of telling your family that they are special to you. Don't save the nice dishes and linen for company only. Sunday dinner, even if it is sandwiches, should be served graciously. Sunday is a special day.

When planning a meal, try to combine foods that can be ready at the same time. This takes practice. Be sure everything you need is on the table before you are seated so you don't have to keep bobbing up and down. Clear off everything except the dessert cutlery and water glasses if you have dessert. Friday night is usually buffet night at our home. By then, everyone is ready for a more relaxed, casual meal. Especially mom. Always consider the comfort and convenience of those you are serving.

Cleaning Up

At last! If you have tidied as you cooked, washing pots and dishes, putting things away, wiping up spills, cleanup will be simple. Even in the mornings, if you are dashing off to work, do the dishes before leaving. It will take just a few minutes, and when you come home a clean kitchen is so much nicer than dirty dishes dried on the table.

Do not leave the kitchen after dinner until the leftovers are put away, the dishes done, the floor swept, and the table and chairs put in their proper places.

There, you're finished. Great feeling, isn't it?

10

Having a Baby

There are very few sentences in the human vocabulary which are laden with more hope and anticipation than the declaration, "We are going to have a baby!"

Probably every little girl at some time has rocked a doll, a cat, or some other object, pretending that it was a baby. Is it instinctive for a girl to want to be a mother?

You are fortunate, as you are about to realize the fulfillment of your destiny as a woman — to be a mother in Zion.

Your coming motherhood may have been apparent to you in one of these ways: You throw up every morning. All day you feel queasy, then you throw up each evening right along with the five o'clock news. You pass so much water so frequently that you dare not get out of bathroom range. You keep falling asleep — anytime, anywhere. Your breasts are sore. At first you were sure it was cancer. Seemingly minor things can make you laugh or cry. You are craving all those funny foods you used to tease your mother about — the ice cream at midnight, and the pretzels, pizzas, and pickles. Worst and most baffling of all, you can't tolerate the smell of your husband's shaving lotion, toothpaste, deodorant, or, at times, him.

Most of you are excited and happy, very happy. But not all of you feel that way, at least not yet. A few of you have reservations about becoming a mother, and you are experiencing guilt because you think the "right" reaction is one of joy.

I'm not sure there is a right reaction. Every woman has her own particular circumstances and feelings. Perhaps you feel disbelief. ("Who, me? I can't be pregnant, not me.") Do you feel dismay? ("Already? Of course I want a baby, but so soon?") Are you afraid? ("What if something goes wrong? Will I miscarry? What about those allergy pills I've been taking? I'm Rh negative, he's Rh positive.") Perhaps you are worried. ("Will the baby be normal? Am I capable of being a good mother? Will the baby come between my husband and me? How will he like being a father? Can we afford a baby? Will my nonmember husband want him to be blessed?") Or maybe you are feeling selfish and a twinge of resentment. ("My figure will be ruined. There goes my freedom. I'll have to quit my job, and I love my job.")

Don't be too hard on yourself. Having a baby is a very serious matter with great consequences, lifelong responsibilities, and eternal implications. It cannot be taken lightly.

But don't get bogged down in the negative aspects of it either, for there are many if you look for them. Instead, think of the gospel-oriented perspective, and realize the significance of the process you are now involved in.

Think of it. You are about to provide a mortal body for one of God's spirit children, "a heavenly aristocrat . . . wise, good, accomplished, ancient beyond conception . . . traveling incognito in your care." (In a personal letter from Dr. Carlfred B. Broderick, 10 June 1980.) And by so doing you become a part of the endless line of women which includes your own mother, grandmother, and Mary, mother of the Christ, and Eve, the first mother of this earth.

You are participating in God's major purpose, "to bring to pass the immortality and eternal life of man" (Moses 1:39). As the profundity of this penetrates your soul, share it with your husband. This will add to the spirituality of your pregnancy and subsequent motherhood.

It's a good thing that Heavenly Father, in his wisdom, has given you nine months in which to prepare yourself physically, mentally, emotionally, and spiritually to be a mother. This is a time of growth, not only of the child's body and your stomach, but also of your spirit, your understanding, and your sense of commitment. This call to be a mother is the greatest call you'll ever get.

During this waiting period, observe, study, pray, and learn what a real mother is, what a family is, and what the needs of an infant are. Consider how you are going to meet these varied needs. How you will stay close to your husband and help him feel a vital part in all of this. Think of what talents and aptitude you have which you might develop to enable you to be effective as a mother.

And while it is true that pregnancy is not a disease but rather a perfectly normal process, it does place a tremendous stress on your body and mind. This can lead to distress. Try not to allow yourself to fall into self-pity. Try not to become a self-centered invalid. Try to stay cheerful and accept your discomforts gracefully. It will be a lot more fun for you and everyone around you if you do.

I would be the last person to suggest that having a baby is simple. It is not easy. Still, so much depends on your own attitude. Be optimistic. Smile.

There are lots of other ways to counteract the stresses and discomforts of pregnancy. Here are a few ideas. Draw on both your testimony and your sense of humor to find the positives hidden in every situation. Strengthen your body through continued exercise, a balanced diet, lots of rest, good posture, and plenty of fresh air. Enjoy the maternity fashions, and know that a pregnant woman, however big and awkward, is beautiful in a special way. Stay involved in life as much as your health will allow.

Show extra consideration and kindness to your husband. He is new at this, too, and likely has his own insecurities. Communicate openly with him. Share everything. This can be a precious time of dreaming about your little family, the trumpets and ballet shoes, the two-wheelers, missions and temple weddings. Once the baby is born, you will have fewer long, quiet, tender evenings alone, so take full advantage of them now.

Prepare the physical necessities for your baby—a place to sleep, bedding, clothing, diapers, etc.

Go to a reputable doctor that you feel you can trust. See him as often as he advises and follow his instructions.

For most of you, the time will zip by without any major complications. Some of you will even feel better and look more radiant than you normally do.

Others of you will encounter some problems. You may be sick

for the first three months, six months, or for the whole nine months. You may have latent problems that flare up from the extra stress to your body—diabetes, high blood pressure, back pain, swollen legs, or itchy skin.

And, unfortunately, some of you will have the kinds of complications that result in the termination of your pregnancy in miscarriage. It can happen at any time, but it usually occurs within the first trimester. At any time, it is traumatic to lose a baby.

Many things can trigger a miscarriage. It may be due to trouble within the embryo or the mother. If your family has a history of miscarried babies, alert your doctor to it and he may be able to prevent it.

If you have never studied the development of a fetus, go to your library and get some medical books or a guide written by a doctor, and read it with your husband. When I consider the formation of a human baby, I can't think of language that is adequate to describe it.

Within hours of conception, the sex of your child is determined along with all its hereditary characteristics of hair and eye color, skin tone, height, and all the rest. This information is in the chromosomes contained in your ovum and his sperm.

In about a week this original little cell set has divided and multiplied many times over and has made its way down into your uterus. There it becomes attached or implanted on the wall, where it will remain until birth.

I can understand cell division, which results in more cells of the same kind. That is logical. What boggles my mind is the fact that after a certain period the cells do not all remain the same. They specialize.

Some cells form the placenta, while others become the umbilical cord, brains, heart, bones, hair, fingers, and whatever else it takes to make a person. That is utterly amazing. Miraculous.

The speed with which all of this happens is also impressive. By the time you realize you're pregnant that little clump of cells has become an embryo with the beginnings of a brain, the major organs, backbone, ears, and eyes, though the entire embryo is only about 2/10 inches long.

At the end of the first trimester when the nausea presumably stops, the fetus, as it is now called, is recognizable as a tiny three-inch long human being with its organs, fingers, and toes. It weighs only one ounce. Meanwhile, on the outside, you aren't even showing yet.

In the next six months the fetus continues to grow and develop, refining all its parts preparatory to separating from your body and living in a new environment.

During the fifth month the fetus becomes big enough so its movements can be felt by you. At first it is only a flutter, but just before delivery it may feel more like a stampede. Our last baby was so active that the older children named him "Thumper" as they felt his gyrations.

So much for what is happening to junior; what is happening to you is pretty fascinating, too.

Two hormones, progesterone and estrogen, are at work helping your body to adapt to its new task. Particularly noteworthy is the effect of progesterone. It causes your involuntary or smooth muscles to relax. This is vital in the uterus and the blood vessels. If the uterus wasn't relaxed, it could not stretch to accommodate the fetus. By nature, the uterus is a strong, tight muscle.

Then, when you consider that your blood supply increases by about 40 percent during pregnancy, you can see why the blood vessels would need to relax. You will even be able to see the veins in your breasts as extra blood is supplied there to help get the milk supply ready for your baby.

Your body is constructed to carry out this intricate and complicated process. Who says men and women are alike?

As time passes and you approach your due date, if your doctor doesn't recommend a prenatal clinic for you and your husband, ask about one. It can be both reassuring and helpful.

Finally, the day will come when you get those signals that tell you the waiting is almost over: dull back pain, some blood show, membranes that leak or rupture, contractions of varying severity and regularity.

This stage can last a short time, or it may take many hours. It is an exciting time but also a scary time because there is always the fear that something may be wrong. But as you have done throughout the nine months, be optimistic. You are about to participate in a wonderful experience.

The contractions indicate that two things are happening to make the birth possible. The uterus which has been relaxed and continually expanding for several months, now begins to tighten from the top down, forcing the baby toward the birth canal. At the same time, the cervix is being softened and opened to allow the baby to pass through.

When all the systems are set at *go,* you will get a strong sensation of wanting to bear down. The doctor will check to make sure everything is ready and then will tell you to push. You will feel pressure, and then if you watch, you will see a tiny head emerge, followed by the tiny shoulders. Then with a rush the rest of the body will glide out.

Again, I can't accurately describe the feeling I had at that particular moment. There is no pain, just an utter relief as an encompassing peace washes over you. You will be acutely aware that you have just witnessed a miracle. It will be a moment you will cherish all your life.

As the doctor hands you your baby, you will see her dear face for the first time. She will lay trustingly against you. You become aware of her warmth, her breathing, her softness. You look into your husband's tear-filled eyes, and you know there are angels in the room. God, himself, is very near. Both of you feel a prayer well up in your heart.

There you are, your husband, your child, and you, together for the first time as a distinct family unit. The eternal bonding has begun.

11

Being the Mother

Much of the talk in the world today indicates that staying at home with children is "boring, intellectually crippling, limiting, and unrewarding."

What do you think? Perhaps you have given up an interesting job for this. Will you be disappointed? Will being a mother be a letdown? What actually do you know about being a mother?

Have you taken a course in motherhood? Do you have a license stating that you are qualified to be a mother?

Sometimes our world doesn't make much sense, does it? You cannot be an electrician, plumber, nurse, teacher, or hairdresser unless you take a prescribed course and have the papers to prove you've passed requirements.

Yet to be a mother all you need is the basic equipment you were born with and reception of a spermatazoon. At least, that's all you need to be a biological mother.

But what does it take to be a *real* mother, one who is effective in her role?

Motherhood isn't something with one definite definition. It isn't just a coat you slip on as soon as your baby is born. Rather, it's more like the process of warping the loom, thread by thread, then learning to weave, and after years of practice, failures, and continued application, finally beginning to see some fabric emerging as a result of your consistent, persistent efforts.

Being a mother covers a lot of territory over a long period of time. Giving birth, feeding, bathing, and clothing your child are certainly part of motherhood, but they represent only a small segment of the overall responsibility and opportunity that are now yours.

Nearly every mother starts out much as you have, with a sweet little baby, no experience, no structured training, lots of insecurity, and great hopes for becoming a good mother.

Since there is no prescribed mothering course, I want to suggest that you build and pursue such a program on your own.

You have access to direct counsel from he who knows the whole course. Study the scriptures as well as the messages of Church leaders.

You will probably feel inadequate as you read and study these things because you feel you don't measure up to everything you are learning. Perfection is constantly presented to you as a goal. It is there to let you know what you are working toward. The purpose is not to make you feel guilty but to show you what is possible.

Know that you can't do everything at once, but you certainly can do something. Pick out the areas which you are going to work on at any given time. Then later, you might move on to something else. Work at it like a weaver; learn, try, improve, progress a bit at a time. You can't achieve it all at once, but you can a little at a time.

To start, *make* fifteen minutes available every day at more or less the same time for reading the scriptures or modern messages from Church leaders. I know you've heard that all your life, but now, more than ever, you *need* the blessings that result from such a regular study pattern. Busy or not, this is vital.

We are familiar with the idea of being too busy sawing to take time to sharpen the saw. I believe that daily scripture study is one way to sharpen the saw.

Only after you stick with the scriptures for a prolonged time will some of these benefits become apparent.

You will find specific answers to your specific questions. You will grow spiritually as you learn the commandments and strive to keep them. The Spirit will filter through every aspect of your daily life, adding depth, insight, and flashes of pure knowledge to uplift you when you need it. You will have peace of mind knowing you are being obedient to the prophet's counsel to study the scriptures daily. These few minutes will be as a pool of serenity in an otherwise hectic and fragmented day. You will realize better results from your other efforts — like sawing with a sharpened saw.

I have a testimony of the great value of regular, daily scripture study. I know it will help you to be a happier, more effective wife and mother.

Daily prayer is another essential tool for a mother. I think that the Lord expects us to do as he counseled Oliver Cowdery to do in D&C 9:

> Behold, you have not understood; you have supposed that I would give it unto you, when you took no thought save it was to ask me.
>
> But, behold, I say unto you, that you must study it out in your mind; then you must ask me if it be right, and if it is right I will cause that your bosom shall burn within you; therefore, you shall feel that it is right.
>
> But if it be not right you shall have no such feelings, but you shall have a stupor of thought that shall cause you to forget the thing which is wrong. (D&C 9:7-9.)

We must do all we can rather than just expect the Lord to automatically grant us full answers to our needs. After we have exhausted our own resources, then we can feel good about asking him for help.

Don't hesitate to seek out the best books on the subject of child-rearing. Perhaps you do not trust books by psychologists and pediatric specialists and would rather go it alone on the premise that love alone is all your child needs.

There is no question in my mind that the single most important factor in child-rearing is an attitude of love and acceptance. I agree that this is far more significant than the skills, techniques, and psychological material propounded by the so-called experts.

But learning what children of certain ages, in general, are prone to think, do, and feel will give you a greater understanding of your particular child.

Often when I have been at my wits' end with the behavior of a child, I have turned to books which counsel parents on raising children. Many times in the wee morning hours I have anxiously reread what experts had to say about children of a certain age.

Most times I have put the books back with a quick prayer of "Thanks, he's just normal," and gone to sleep, relieved of a great burden. Knowing what you might expect from your children can definitely make motherhood less traumatic.

I also feel that correct phrases and discipline skills are less important than a basic attitude of wanting to understand. But, again, I feel that learning how you might handle typical situations will give you confidence in coping with your own children.

Sister Camilla Kimball told sisters at an area conference: "The role of mother is the most exacting and difficult of all professions. A woman should, therefore, be skilled in child training, in psychology and sociology, in economics and management, in nutrition and nursing. She should seek a well-rounded education."

So study, go to classes, and gain all the background knowledge you can. This, coupled with the scriptures, prayer, common sense, and inspiration will make you equal to your task.

Ultimately, you and your husband have full responsibility for your children, so you must become the "experts" regarding them. Do not get too dependent on the opinions and advice of others. Not even a noted child psychologist can really know your particular child and your home as well as you do.

The Lord has outlined basic principles for raising children. And as always you may choose whether to follow his instructions or not.

For those who have chosen to be obedient, the next question is, what are these principles?

Love Your Children

"That they may teach the young women to be sober, to love their husbands, to love their children." (Titus 2:4.)

Teach Them the Gospel by Precept and Example

"And again, inasmuch as parents have children in Zion, or in any of her stakes which are organized, that teach them not to understand the doctrine of repentance, faith in Christ the son of the living God, and of baptism and the gift of the Holy Ghost by the laying on of the hands, when eight years old, the sin be upon the heads of the parents." (D&C 68:25.)

From the life of President Hugh B. Brown comes a sterling example of a mother teaching her son to know and trust God:

> I remember my mother said to me when I went on my mission in 1904. . . . "My boy, you are going a long ways away from me now. Do you remember," she said, "that when you were a little lad you used to have bad dreams and get frightened? Your bedroom was just off mine, and frequently you would cry out in the night and say, 'Mother, are you there?' and I would answer 'Yes, my boy, I'm here — everything is all right. Turn over and go to sleep.' You always did. Knowing that I was there gave you courage.
>
> "Now," she said, "You will be about 6,000 miles away, and though you may cry out for me I cannot answer you." She added this, "There is one who can, and if you call to him, he'll hear you when you call. He will respond to your appeal. You just say, 'Father, are you there?' and there will come into your heart the comfort and solace such as you knew as a boy when I answered you." (Leon R. Hartshorn, *Memories of Mothers by General Authorities*, Deseret Book Co., 1971, page 7.)

Look to Their Spiritual, Physical, Social-Emotional, and Intellectual Needs

"And ye will not suffer your children that they go hungry, or naked; neither will ye suffer that they transgress the laws of God, and fight and quarrel one with another, and serve the devil, who is the master of sin, or who is the evil spirit which hath been spoken of by our fathers, he being an enemy to all righteousness. But ye will teach them to walk in the ways of truth and soberness; ye will teach them to love one another, and to serve one another." (Mosiah 4:14-15.)

"All children have claim upon their parents for their maintenance until they are of age." (D&C 83:4.)

Discipline and Restrain Them

"And ye fathers, provoke not your children to wrath: but bring them up in the nurture and admonition of the Lord." (Ephesians 6:4.)

"Reproving betimes with sharpness, when moved upon by the Holy Ghost; and then showing forth afterwards an increase of love toward him whom thou hast reproved, lest he esteem thee to be his enemy." (D&C 121:43.)

Respect Them: The Lord Loves Them

"Behold your little ones. And as they looked to behold they cast their eyes towards heaven, and they saw the heavens open, and they saw angels descending out of heaven as it were in the midst of fire; and they came down and encircled those little ones about, and they were encircled about with fire; and the angels did minister unto them." (3 Nephi 17:23-24.)

"And now, he imparteth his word by angels unto men, yea, not only men but women also. Now this is not all; little children do have words given unto them many times which confound the wise and the learned." (Alma 32:23.)

Enjoy Them

"Lo, children are an heritage of the Lord: and the fruit of the womb is his reward. As arrows are in the hand of a mighty man; so are children of the youth. Happy is the man that hath his quiver full of them." (Psalm 127:3-5.)

That includes just about everything, doesn't it? How can any mother do everything? Fortunately, you are not alone in the assignment. The Lord planned that each child should have two parents who would help and support each other in the over-whelming challenge of raising their children.

Now that you know *what* the task of motherhood is, you would probably like to know *how* to do it, right?

I wish I could just lay out a pattern for you to follow that would result in happy, well-adjusted, spiritual children; but of course, that is not possible. I can offer specific ideas that you may want to incorporate into your mothering fabric.

My concern is not to have you do things the way I did, but rather to have you discover your own best way to be the kind of mother you want to be.

So, go through these and pick out whatever feels right for you, and don't worry about the ones that don't.

You, the Mother

When you have an awful day, know that every mother alive has days like that. You are one of us. When things do go wrong, repentance and rededication are to be preferred over discouragement and depression. But if you do get depressed, admit it; then seek help. Don't be embarrassed. Don't feel guilty. Do take steps to overcome it.

Treasure the happy days when you feel great, your baby stays on schedule, and you have dinner on the table when your husband comes home.

Enjoy your newborn babies. Give yourself to them as totally as you can. In about six months your baby will settle into some sort of routine and you can resume a schedule of your own. Discuss this with your husband. See if he will agree to a flexible life-style that revolves around the baby's needs for this short season. It would be a good investment.

Know that each mother will like different aspects of the total mothering spectrum. The old saying, "The early years are the best years," is not true for all. Some of you will like the later years better.

Even if you can't be home full time, you can still be a dedicated, loving mother.

"Mother sets the tone of the home" is true; unfair perhaps, but true. Cultivate a cheerful and optimistic outlook even in the face of daily disasters like allergies, late dinners, diarrhea, sticky floors, and no clean diapers.

Do not try to derive your sense of worth from your children. Cultivate your self-esteem within yourself.

Try not to worry about what others think and say about how you and your husband are raising your family. Also, do not presume to judge others.

Arrange with your husband or a good friend for some regular time out each week.

Develop an attitude of appreciation. Even minor, everyday things like seventeen wilted dandelions with droopy heads, or a husband who bathes a little son, can add greatly to your happiness if you will accept them as special gifts. So much depends on your attitude.

Be courteous to your husband and the children. Some parents treat strangers nicer than they do their own family.

As your children get older and have ideas of their own, make a point to listen, trying to understand their point of view. Do not assume that you are right all of the time. And be tolerant. Children will be childish.

Be completely honest with your family. Do not sneak out on a toddler to avoid a crying scene. If he should waken while you are gone, his confidence in you will be shaken.

More than any other characteristic, you will need to develop patience. Learn to bite your tongue and wait a few minutes for the flash of anger to pass. You'll be glad you did. You are better able to be reasonable if you do this.

Long-range patience is also necessary. Even a colicky baby will stop crying some day, nearly every child who starts grade one is fully toilet trained, and even the spookiest boy grows up to leave his night light and blanket at home when he goes on his mission.

Be ever prayerful. You will need all the added help you can get, so study and pray regularly to stay in tune.

Try to remember that Heavenly Father loves your youngsters as much as you do. Trust him.

Develop emotional maturity. Be willing to sacrifice some of your wants and needs for the good of the family.

Keep your sense of humor alive. Keep a record of the things your children do or say which give you "a joy." Here are samples from my journal:

> "There's a famine in our fridge, mom."
> "Shut your mouths everybody, we're going by the dentist's office."
> "May I have some clean soup (broth), please?"
> "These scissors (pinking shears) have teeth!"
> "Those are Dalmation (Holstein) cows."

Children can be exasperating, but if you can keep your sense of humor it is easier. "Show me a child in a snowsuit and I'll show you a child who needs to go to the bathroom."

Relating to Your Husband

Do at least one special thing for your husband each week to let him know that, although the baby takes up much of your time, he is still number one in your life. Express your love and appreciation often.

Encourage him to share himself with the children and to feel good about himself as a father.

When the children are very small explain to them that their father is gone so much because he is working to earn money so he can buy them food, shoes, and toys. Tell them he is doing this because he loves them.

Tell them that you also love their dad, and then treat him in such a way that reinforces the message.

Request that he use his priesthood in giving blessings to the children or yourself when needed.

Support and sustain him as the head of the house, whether he has the priesthood or not.

Never ridicule or belittle your husband in front of the children. Do not compete with him for their affection, either. This is a co-operative effort, not a competition.

Relating to Your Children

Love each child unconditionally. Regardless of how he looks, or what he says or does, you must let him know that you still love him. When a child seems to least deserve your love he needs it the most.

Show sincere interest in each child as an individual. Do not compare one to another. Listen, observe, and interact with each one noting likes, dislikes, fears, and wishes; you will see the magic of personality unfold. This is one of the rewarding aspects of being a mother.

Along with reading readiness for preschoolers, spiritual readiness is equally important. Familiarize them with the religious vocabulary, the names and faces of the First Presidency and Joseph Smith, the basic Bible, Book of Mormon, and Church history stories, and some of the common hymns. In a classroom atmosphere they will appear bright as they know the answers, impress their teachers, and feel good about themselves and the Church. It will influence their attitude toward the Church and the gospel.

Let each child earn some money so he can pay tithing. Be sure to take him to tithing settlement.

Teach your children the basic principles of the gospel in every way you can. Relate the natural joys of life to the love that Heavenly Father has for them. Remember D&C 68:25.

Express your own love for the gospel to your little ones. Let it be part of their daily life as you teach them to associate all the lovely things in the world that you enjoy with the gospel.

Teach your children to be reverent in meetings. At first, this simply means to be quiet, which is very hard for them. Do not let it become a great playtime. It is too hard to rid them of the habit later.

Help your children to associate with each other in a friendly way. Do not tolerate rude behavior toward each other: "neither will ye suffer that they transgress the laws of God, and fight and quarrel one with another, and serve the devil" (Mosiah 4:14).

Set a pattern of loving service within the family. Even though some children do not get along as well with one as they do with another, they still must be taught to show respect and consideration for each other. Different does not mean inferior.

Do not allow verbal or physical abuse to ever get started in your home.

Encourage everyone in your family to express his real feelings, even the negative ones. Create an atmosphere of security in which all feel safe and accepted.

Take children seriously. Some adults consider children carefree. I do not agree. I think most children are aware of the world around them and are trying to figure it out. If your child casually asks, "Does it hurt to die?" do not put him off with some flippant answer such as, "You shouldn't be worrying about things like that," or, "Don't be silly. You will be with your Heavenly Father." Translate the fear and concern expressed in his questions to your own level. Then answer him at his level. He needs reassurance that means something to him. How about, "You know that daddy and I love you, don't you? In heaven you also have a father and a mother. They loved you even before we had you. They and lots of spirit brothers and sisters are waiting for you to come back from your big trip to earth. They will want to know all about it. What will you tell them?"

Your degree of influence with children in later years will largely depend on the kind of relationship that you build now. Consciously build a loving, trusting relationship with each child by communicating freely, spending time together, teaching, playing, working, worshipping, and laughing.

Child proof your home as much as possible by putting caustic cleaners, insecticides, medicines and sharp objects out of sight and reach. Children are constantly exploring their environment and will try anything at least once. Prevention is much more desirable than attempted cures.

Enrich your home environment in every way to stimulate your children to find their talents and to develop them. Home should be a place of fun, learning, and excitement. Do not let the feeling develop that you must go out or have someone in to have fun. Create a camaraderie within the family. Family home evening is marvelous for this. Television will sap up the hours unless you provide interesting alternatives. We use books, games, puzzles, music, projects, and study in the home plus excursions, outings, gardening, and dinner out once a month to keep creativity and fun alive as a family.

Let small children help when they want to or they won't when you want them to. It is good to establish a helping pattern, even if it means having a sink drain clogged by the six knives your helper forces down there.

Make a conscious effort to develop a healthy self-concept in each child. Reassure him of his worth. Give him confidence in his abilities. Encourage him to find his strengths and build on them. Help him to accept his limitations and cope with them. A mother has great affect on how a child sees himself. The impression often remains through his whole life.

Never underestimate a child. Some adults look down on children. But children are often far more intelligent and perceptive than adults give them credit for. All they lack is experience. Ever hear the saying, "Some men never overcome the ignorance of their mothers"?

Be realistic but maintain high expectations for them. You already know that people pretty well act and perform to the level expected of them. Do not hamper your child with a load of negative attitudes.

Recognize that failure is as much a part of living as is breathing. Teach by example and precept to take it in stride and to keep trying. Never label a child as being lazy or stupid. He will believe you.

Do not try to completely shield a child from the evils of the world. You may succeed for six years but then he must go out into the world when school starts. Prepare him by exposing him to what he might encounter, and teach him how to cope with it so that when he is tempted to steal, lie, cheat, or take the Lord's name in vain, he will not be caught up in the newness and excitement of it. He will already know that it is not acceptable. It's immunization against immorality.

Help your child to know that nonmembers are not wicked because they smoke or drink. Teach him to respect others.

Discipline

Many consider discipline to be a negative force only. Ideally, however, it is training by instruction and control to produce improvement.

Discuss discipline with your husband and determine how it will be used in your home. If you have differences along the way, settle them privately while presenting a united front to the children. If you do not support each other, they will learn to pit you against each other.

Not even God would ever force a child. Remember, "only by persuasion, by long-suffering, by gentleness and meekness, and by love unfeigned; by kindness and pure knowledge, which shall greatly enlarge the soul without hypocrisy, and without guile." (D&C 121:41-42.) In any case, you cannot force children to love and respect you. This you must earn.

Respect each child's free agency, but do not use it as an excuse for not teaching him correct principles. You must first teach him the gospel and help him to see what the consequences of various behaviors are. Then let him use his agency. The Prophet Joseph Smith said, "I teach the people correct principles, and they govern themselves."

A few firm rules consistently and firmly enforced will do more for order and harmony than will a whole sheaf of rules. As the children get older include them in family councils to determine the rules. They are more likely to support and even help to enforce rules which they help to set.

Learn to separate actions from personalities. Bad behavior does not make the child bad. Do not get caught in the web of threats and bribes, and stay out of power struggles. Do not make promises unless you intend to keep them.

Use positive messages often, even for correction. "No, you may not go to Billy's today, but you may help mix up the cookies."

Know that verbal correction alone is ineffective on a small child. Combine the verbal message with a physical one. "You must not touch the lamp," needs to be accompanied by actually lifting the child away from the lamp. After repetition the two messages will blend, and he will understand when you tell him to leave the lamp alone. He learns to obey. But if you just yell "No, no," he becomes disobedient by default.

Give much positive attention to a well-behaved child.

Do not reward negative behavior like whining, begging, or temper tantrums. Try to anticipate needs before the child has to demand them.

A quiet voice is a great asset.

Every child needs and wants the security of limits, lovingly imposed and enforced consistently by his parents.

Be willing to admit when you are wrong, and apologize.

The surest way to make a child miserable is to always give him everything he thinks he wants and to let him do anything he feels like. There is no anticipation or surprise in a life of total indulgence.

Try to make necessary daily routines, such as bedtime, enjoyable. If they are fun, children will not cause an unpleasant scene every day.

Mealtime should be pleasant, not a time for pitting your will against a child's.

Natural consequences are great teachers and should be allowed to run their course, except when the consequence could be fatal.

Then logical consequences must be substituted. "Running into the street is dangerous. You could get hit by a car. Since you insist on running into the street, you must come into the house." With that, pick up the child and take him inside.

Encourage independence, let children make up their own minds, face the consequences of their behavior, and cope with their problems. Over-protection cripples children. They become dependent, weak, and unhappy adults.

And finally, as necessary as discipline is, do not forget the great value of tenderness and mercy. There is not much of either left in this world, and if a child does not get them from his mother, he may miss them altogether.

Of course, this is not all that is involved in being a mother. Things will come up in your home that no one else has ever experienced; each life is unique. There will be many similar experiences as well. There will be some grim days which make you cry as you think of President David O. McKay's statement, "No other success can compensate for failure in the home."

At those times, remember this companion statement by President Harold B. Lee, "No home is a failure as long as that home doesn't give up." (Harold B. Lee, "Maintain Your Place as a Woman," *Ensign,* February 1972, page 56.) Further, Elder Neal A. Maxwell has counseled us to be aware "that because the home is so crucial, it will be the source of our greatest failures as well as our greatest joys." (Neal A. Maxwell, "The Value of Home Life," *Ensign,* February 1972, page 7.)

Every one of you will have successes and failures in your home.

When you feel like the bottom is about to fall out, take your husband's hand and go stand by the cribs of your sleeping babies. Don't say anything. Just stand there and look at those peaceful children. As you do, a healing wave of love and tenderness will wash over you. A sleeping child is one of the rewards you receive for being a parent, a mother.

There are lots of rewards, not to be calculated in dollars, sprinkled throughout your days: the trusting look of an infant; a delighted gurgle; a drowsy head snuggled against your shoulder; a small hand clutching your little finger; a two-year-old saying his very own prayer; a three-year-old son gently caressing the hands and feet on a picture of the Savior as he murmurs, "Sore"; a five-year-old who bursts in from kindergarten, "You know what, today we got to draw our favorite thing, and I drew you!"

By now you must know that I am not one of the people who labels motherhood as "boring, intellectually crippling, limiting, or unrewarding." I believe it is the most significant human development career in the world, for it develops not only a child but also a mother.

As the mother, you are both the filter and the magnifying glass for your children as they explore and experience the gospel and the world. Your role is vital.

Think now of the stripling warriors in Alma 56. They were just young men, teenagers. They had not been trained as warriors, but they went into battle to protect their families and homes. They were fearless: "Now they never had fought, yet they did not fear death; and they did think more upon the liberty of their fathers than they did upon their lives; yea, they had been taught by their mothers, that if they did not doubt, God would deliver them. And they rehearsed unto me the words of their mothers, saying: We do not doubt our mothers knew it." (Alma 56:47-48.)

Such can be the influence of a mother.

12

Trials

"Yet man is born unto trouble" (Job 5:7), and "it must needs be, that there is an opposition in all things." (2 Nephi 2:11.)

Why?

"My son, peace be unto thy soul: thine adversity and thine afflictions shall be but a small moment; and then, if thou endure it well, God shall exalt thee on high." (D&C 121:7-8.)

None of this is new to you, is it? You've heard it all many times. Still, you, like many others, probably don't really expect that troubles and adversities will happen to you. "No, not me. Things like that always happen to others." Right?

Inevitably problems do arise in everyone's life. And when they do there are often comments such as: "Why me? What did I do to deserve this? I go to my meetings. I pay my tithing, I support the brethren. Why is this happening to me?" And the stock answer is, "For whom the Lord loveth he chasteneth, and scourgeth every son whom he receiveth." (Hebrews 12:6.)

Does that answer bother you?

It bothered me for years. I could never figure out why the Lord would want to make life difficult for those he loved. That didn't make any sense. When you pray, do you ask for hardships? Don't you usually ask for health and strength, love and harmony, peace and safety?

As I've thought about this over the years, I've come to have some ideas about Hebrews 12:6, though I certainly don't pretend to fully understand the total implications.

One parallel that helps me is to think of the violin, a tremendously versatile instrument. It can produce beautiful music, but only if there is stress or pressure applied to its strings. When the strings are totally relaxed, the music produced is sloppy, unmelodious, and monotonous.

Think of a championship basketball game. Suppose your team is "psyched up" and anxious to play another top team in a playoff. Imagine the tension and the excitement. The adrenalin is really flowing.

Then the opposing team comes thundering onto the floor, looking sharp and exuding competence and confidence as they take their warm-up shots. Their practice period is impressive, even intimidating.

Finally, the whistle blows to signal the start of the game. Instead of taking their starting positions for the tip-off, their whole team lines up along center court with folded arms. No one moves.

Your team mills around nervously. Finally, the officials call the game. You have won by default because the opposing team refuses to oppose you. The championship is yours. You have won; but it is a hollow victory. You feel no excitement, no satisfaction, no joy —just a tremendous letdown, for it is more satisfying to play and be defeated than to not play at all.

It's true that life is not a game, but I think there is a valid comparison here. If the Lord granted you smooth, no-challenge days, with steak and apple pie as constant fare, he would not be giving you joy and happiness; he would be giving you boredom and misery. That is what I think. How about you?

Whenever I try to picture that kind of life, the image of a cow, placidly chewing her cud as she sits in a grassy meadow shaded by tall poplars, keeps flashing across my mind.

Does that bovine pastoral existence appeal to you?

Our purpose for being here on earth is not to be coddled in a life of ease, but to be tried and tested in every imaginable way so we can learn to meet problems, gain knowledge, develop skills, and find solutions. We are expected to develop ourselves so that, no matter what, we are able to endure, keep the faith, and be found worthy to return to that Father who sent us here.

The Lord has outlined: "I will prove you in all things, whether you will abide in my covenant, even unto death, that you may be found worthy. For if ye will not abide in my covenant ye are not worthy of me." (D&C 98:14-15.)

That is a big challenge.

Let's examine adversity for a moment. Identification and classification may help us to better know what we face.

Trials seem to fit into three general categories.

Trials Which Are Natural or Logical Consequences

If you break a commandment, you will suffer the consequences—anguish, pain, guilt, whatever. If you are driving through an intersection on a green light and someone comes plowing through on a red, both of you will suffer the consequences. If you lay on the beach for five sunny hours, you will get burned.

Inescapable Everyday Risks

These are risks that are ever present, and by the sheer law of averages, now and again you are going to suffer the effects of some of them. You are bound to pick up a flu bug, cold virus, or other illness because the germs and viruses are present in the air you breathe. If you are allergic to pollen, whenever it is present you will suffer the symptoms of that allergy.

Natural or Unexplained Events

Some trials are usually unexpected, unearned, and unwelcome. No one causes them, and they cannot be rightly termed a part of daily life. The eruption of Mount St. Helens in Washington caused severe adversity to many. Sudden hail and wind storms cause widespread property damage. Many die suddenly from rare disease or unexpected illness.

Regardless of the cause, adversity creates a disruptive or disquieting influence on your life. Pain is pain, whether it results from a consequence of what you or someone else did, from a common daily hazard, or from a natural disaster. It still hurts.

Elder Marvin J. Ashton said: "Adversity will surface in some form in every life. How we prepare for it, how we meet it, makes the difference. We can be broken by adversity, or we can become stronger. The final result is up to the individual." (Marvin J. Ashton, "Adversity and You," *Ensign,* November 1980, page 54.)

Every life will have trials, even yours. There is no question about that. The only questions are what kind, when, and how will you cope with them?

Perhaps it would be wise to consider the kinds of adversities that are most likely to arise in your life. "If ye are prepared ye shall not fear." (D&C 38:30.)

Human relationship problems. Because of the constant, intensely emotional associations within a family, there can be great misery as well as great happiness. You may encounter friction with your husband, children, and in-laws — both your parents and his.

Illness or injury. Prolonged illness or injury to you is particularly challenging because the rest of the family depends on you. Any illness or injury in the family will cause added stress, worry, extra work, perhaps loss of income, loss of sleep, and often an inability to keep things going.

Death of a loved one. Miscarriage is very disappointing. Death of people you have had a long association with is heartbreaking. Some feel it a sign of weakness or lack of faith if one is upset and cries at death. Death is always a tragedy to those who are left behind.

The gospel definitely takes the desperation out of death, but it does not erase the sorrow. Recently I heard this quote at a funeral, "The only way to take sorrow out of death is to take love out of life." Bitter and prolonged grief, however, would belie the gospel.

Husband's frequent absences. In your early married years, your husband may be gone to study or work long hours to establish his career so he will be better able to support you and the children. He may also be gone because of sports or other recreation. Or he may be gone on Church assignments.

Wavering testimony. A wavering testimony is serious for anyone, but especially for a mother because her attitudes affect the whole family. Also, the demands on her life are so intense that she needs the sweet, steadying influence of a strong testimony.

Lack of personal development, identity, and motivation. It is easy for you to get so involved in caring for your family, filling Church duties, and giving service, that you neglect your own needs. This kind of sacrifice is admirable. But it needs to be tempered with some filling and refreshing times for yourself.

Exhaustion. Whether you have a student husband or one who has to work long hours, and a baby or two or three, you may find that being totally worn out is your major problem.

Repetition and lack of control. No matter how completely you do your work today, it will all be waiting for you again tomorrow. In addition, so much of what happens is out of your control — the baby gets a fever, he spills a whole bottle of orange juice on a clean floor, or he falls against the corner of a table.

Fragmentation. There are so many varied demands on your time and energies that if you try to do them all, you begin to feel like you are being divided up into many little parts.

Financial problems. Financial problems can result from a lack of money, mismanagement of funds, or disagreements regarding money.

Depression. Unfortunately, the normal stresses and demands of your life sometimes become excessive, and you, unable to keep coping and smiling, cave in. It may be due to a combination of exhaustion, illness, a tough pregnancy. Or you might have various intense feelings of inadequacy and guilt which finally plunge you into a depression. It makes you feel incapable, hopeless and worthless, and you lose all confidence and incentive. *Get help!*

Well, what do you think? Can you handle it?

Have you ever thought how you might act in a real crisis? It's hard to know, isn't it? Try to think what your reaction would be if you fell against the curb tonight and broke both legs. It's an awful thought, but can you imagine how you might cope with that?

Or look at this adversity-crisis situation from another side: What kind of person would you want to be with if you were caught high up in a mountain pass during a sudden, swirling, blinding blizzard? Would you want to be with someone who went to pieces and cried, was sure you were doomed, thought you'd never get out alive, and complained bitterly that it was unfair and that you might just as well give up because the situation was hopeless?

Or would you like to be with someone who remained calm, optimistic, and worked to figure out how to insure survival and have safe passage down the mountain?

So much depends on attitude and a willingness to face the situation head-on with an eye to solving the problem, doesn't it?

I've outlined below a few ideas of how you might better be able to face the adversities that come to you.

Live every day to the fullest extent, with joy and enthusiasm, gratitude and appreciation. Enjoy your health and freedom, enjoy your family and friends, enjoy the gospel and your routine daily tasks. Then, if they are suddenly diminished or removed entirely, you will not have bitter regrets ("If only I had appreciated what I had when I had it").

Express your love to those dear to you. Write the note, make the phone call, send the flowers before catastrophe intervenes.

Build a strong testimony based on study, service, and prayer. The time will come when you will need it.

Develop an acceptance of the Lord's will. If you get so you want his will more than you want your own, you will be given peace, calm, and dignity even in the face of major trials.

Observe how others face their trials. The memory of a good example can be something to cling to when you are being torn by the rude blasts of adversity.

Read the biography *Spencer W. Kimball.* In fact, read about any of the prophets, ancient or modern. They all were tested very thoroughly. How many years did Jacob have to work to receive Rachel for his wife? And how about the Savior? He didn't have social position or even the comfort of a home; yet, his was the most significant of all lives.

The initial reaction to a major crisis is usually a mixture of disbelief, denial, and self-pity. Do not let yourself get mired down in this initial stage and continue to feel sorry for yourself for any prolonged period.

Make a conscious effort to identify the cause of the pain, and then seek ways to either resolve it or to minimize the disruptive effects of it. Handling or coping with the problem is important. Often when you begin to do something about it, the feelings of hopelessness, helplessness, or panic are brought under control. I asked one young mother, who had a very colicky baby, how she was able to cope with the near-constant crying of her child. She said: "Well, I pray a lot, try to be patient, and I grit my teeth. When it gets really bad, I ask Brent to hold him for a few minutes and I go to another room to just think. Or I read about the pioneers who lost so many babies or watched them be so sick — unable to even shelter them. Then when I take him back, he is a lot more precious to me — crying and all." (Note: The only thing that has changed is her attitude; the baby is still crying.)

When a serious illness or injury restricts your normal routine, ferret out what few things you are still able to do, and then do them. Whatever it is, when you contribute your "mite," you will feel less isolated, less left out, less useless. It will boost your self-concept.

Accept the help and kindness of others graciously.

Stay interested in others. When you are hurting, it is easy to become self-centered. Avoid that.

Help others through their Gethsemanes. "Bear ye one another's burdens, and so fulfil the law of Christ." (Galatians 6:2.)

Develop a sense of perspective ("It could have been worse").

Remind yourself that most crises are temporary. However awful it is right now, in time it will change.

Live one day at a time and determine to live that day well. People who have handicapped children live for years on this basis.

Enumerate the other features of your life which are positive. Even if both your legs are broken, do you still have a loving husband, the use of your hands, a mind that can think, and good friends who visit you? Perspective is important.

Try to keep your sense of humor. Our little son has a "panic button" which his sister got for him at a summer fair. One evening, after a series of frustrating experiences, I was feeling exasperated. This small boy, feeling the tension, took me by the hand and led me to his room where his button was stuck to his wall. With a generous smile, he offered, "You can use my panic button anytime you want, Mom." I hugged him, chuckled, and felt my tension melt away.

Finally, when you reach the end of the trial — your broken legs are healed, you are off the mountain, or your husband gets a job — take time to look back over the period of suffering and lift out one positive product of the experience.

Many such experiences have happened to me, and many have been shared with me by others. I'd like to relate.

Cheryl suffered a severely broken leg which required a seven-pound, full-leg cast for the first four months, much of which time she spent in a wheelchair with her leg elevated. Then she spent almost five more months in lesser casts, and further time on crutches. What could possibly be positive about that?

She says that since her husband had always admired independence, she was afraid that he would get tired of doing his own work, organizing and doing all the housework with the children, and also doing the many personal things for her that she was unable to do for herself. She worried that he might one day say, "This is getting to be a real pain. I've had it."

But, he never did. Instead, he remained infinitely patient and considerate, willingly carrying his tremendous load, day after day, month after month. As she watched him doing all those things she couldn't do for herself, she started to more fully understand that the Savior, likewise, had done for all of us that which we could not do for ourselves.

In reflecting back, she has gained a new appreciation for her husband, her children, and for the Savior. "This sounds crazy, I know, but it was worth it. I don't want to go through it again, but it was definitely worth it." What could be more positive than that?

About twelve years ago one friend and her husband moved all across Canada to Ontario, far from their family and friends. Just before they left their third son was born. It turned out that Michael was extremely handicapped. This friend recently wrote, "Michael's placement in our family made his care very much a family project and probably developed a sense of caring for others in the big boys that they wouldn't have learned in any other way. There was heavy involvement on everyone's part, from the standpoint of helping with Michael as well as cooperating in running the household — a good though not necessarily desirable method of teaching responsibility."

My third reflection was shared with me by a friend whose son contracted a viral infection which totally paralyzed his arms. His mother told him, after some six months of this, "Randy, you don't know how many times I've fasted and prayed asking the Lord to give your affliction to me. I felt I could cope without my arms, and I knew you needed yours." (He is the father of two young children and is in the construction business.)

This wonderful son, still afflicted, said, "Mother, would you have taken this from me and I wouldn't have learned?"

He, along with many others, has become part of that very

special fraternity whose members have discovered that suffering can bring one closer to the Savior.

Trials and adversities, while difficult and distressing, are an important part of mortal life. They force you to exert yourself, to reach, to endure, to find the strength you didn't know you had, and to develop Christlike attributes in yourself. They help you to gain a love and appreciation for Christ, and they illustrate the real meaning of this scripture: "Trust in the Lord with all thine heart; and lean not unto thine own understanding. In all thy ways acknowledge him, and he shall direct thy paths." (Proverbs 3:5-6.)

Remember that even Christ, the literal son of God, was subjected to extreme adversity. "Though he were a Son, yet learned he obedience by the things which he suffered." (Hebrews 5:8.)

That is very special company to be in, don't you agree?

Elder Hugh B. Brown said, "Trouble and adversity, when jointly met, will strengthen the marriage and bind the couple together sometimes more closely than if all the days were sunshine and ease." (*You and Your Marriage*, page 30.)

Happiness is more than the mere absence of pain. Sometimes it is knowing that you have learned to accept the pain and have been able to reach an even higher level of living because of it.

13

The Gospel in Your Home

Did you ever stop to think that the gospel plan and the Church organization are for your individual benefit? That's right. It's all to help you live an abundant life here and qualify for exaltation.

By definition "the word *gospel* means good news. The good news is that Jesus Christ has made the perfect atonement for mankind that will redeem all mankind from the grave and reward each individual according to his/her works." (See Bible Dictionary, *The Holy Bible.*)

"The gospel is a program of action—of doing things. Man's immortality and eternal life are God's goals. (Moses 1:39.) Immortality has been accomplished by the Savior's sacrifice. Eternal life hangs in the balance awaiting the works of men." (Spencer W. Kimball, *The Miracle of Forgiveness,* Bookcraft, 1969, page 208.)

You know the old saying "You can lead a horse to water, but you can't make him drink." Well, that's about how it is with the gospel.

It is all laid out before you. The principles are preached, the ordinances are there, but only you can make them effective in your life. Only you have the power to make that happen.

This is an appeal to each of you as you embark on married life. Make the commitment as did Joshua of ancient times: "Choose you this day whom ye will serve . . . but as for me and my house, we will serve the Lord" (Joshua 24:15).

Some people have told me that the Church expects too much. They say it is demanding, restrictive, and that it makes them feel like music boxes—the tune is set and programmed by the Church, which then winds them up so they will all play the same tune.

I am a convert of twenty years, and as I have studied this gospel and tried to apply it in my own daily life, I have found the opposite to be true. I have found the gospel to be a great liberator. As I've incorporated the basic principles into my life, a whole new, marvelous, and endless vista has opened up before me.

True, the basic melody is set; but instead of rows of music boxes all programmed to play the same arrangement and interpretation of the same tune, I see rows of electronic organs with individuals fiddling with all those switches and keys and pedals that make the many varieties of rhythms, sounds, and beats. Then as each individual sets his organ the way he wants it, he plays the same basic melody line but with his own interpretation and arrangement.

That is how I see the gospel. The basic principles, the commandments, the Articles of Faith, the ordinances are unchangeable; but your individual expression will be just that—individual. There is room in this gospel for everyone.

The gospel of Jesus Christ is a gospel of individual growth, development, and ultimate perfection.

> This progress toward eternal life is a matter of achieving perfection. Living all the commandments guarantees total forgiveness of sins and assures one of exaltation through that perfection which comes by complying with the formula the Lord gave us. In his Sermon on the Mount he made the command to all men: "Be ye therefore perfect, even as your Father which is in heaven is perfect." (Matthew 5:48.) Being perfect means to triumph over sin. This is a mandate from the Lord. He is just and wise and kind. He would never require anything from his children which was not for their benefit and which was not attainable. Perfection therefore is an achievable goal. . . .
>
> Perfection really comes through overcoming. The Lord revealed through John: "To him that overcometh will I grant to sit with me in my throne, even as I also overcame, and am set down with my Father in his throne." (Revelation 3:21.) (*Miracle of Forgiveness,* pages 208-209.)

Truly, living the gospel is an individual responsibility, and the rewards are such that "eye has not seen, nor ear heard, nor yet entered into the heart of man" (D&C 76:10).

Spirituality and eternal life are not commodities which can be purchased in any marketplace. Rather, they must be earned. "There is a law, irrevocably decreed in heaven before the foundations of this world, upon which all blessings are predicated — And when we obtain any blessing from God, it is by obedience to that law upon which it is predicated" (D&C 130:20-21).

Each person must work out her own salvation through study, obedience, prayer, service and being "anxiously engaged in a good cause, and [doing] many things of their own free will, and [bringing] to pass much righteousness" (D&C 58:27).

One specific area of service which I think bears mentioning is that service which we give as we fulfill callings in the Church. There are endless testimonies borne by people who have received tremendous personal development, growth, and testimony by fulfilling the responsibilities to which they have been called.

Certainly there may be unusual circumstances which would prevent you from accepting a call, but I think this would be quite rare. If it should happen to you, then you should surely tell the priesthood leader who calls you. Do not refuse a call just because you don't feel qualified. If everyone did that, there would be many vacant positions.

When President Spencer W. Kimball was first called to be an apostle on July 8, 1943, President J. Reuben Clark phoned him in Arizona and said, "The Brethren have just chosen you to fill one of the vacancies in the Quorum."

President Kimball replied, "Oh, Brother Clark: Not me? You don't mean me? There must be some mistake. . . . I am so weak and small and limited and incapable." (Edward L. Kimball and Andrew E. Kimball, Jr., *Spencer W. Kimball,* Bookcraft, 1977, page 189.)

He accepted, however inadequate he felt, prepared himself as best he was able, and served valiantly as an apostle for thirty years. And, of course, he then became president of the Church.

Each of you will receive many opportunities to serve. Accept the challenge, serve mightily, and you will learn, you will be blessed and strengthened.

I am certainly not an authority by any means, but I am so excited about the way the truths given to us by God can permeate every area of life and give it depth and meaning. Instead of living on the shallow crust of life, you can feast on the fulness, the abundance of life, if you will make the effort.

Do not hold back or make excuses for not going all out; get involved wholeheartedly in the Lord's program. Go to your meetings, study, accept calls, serve others, do your visiting teaching, and be prepared to do all that the Lord expects of you.

Spirituality is a relevant, modern quality; it is not something that should be reserved for little old grandmothers sitting in their rocking chairs reading the scriptures. It is a vital quality which benefits every person.

> The gift of the Holy Ghost adapts itself to all these organs or attributes [of man]. It quickens all the intellectual faculties, increases, enlarges, expands, and purifies all the natural passions and affections, and adapts them, by the gift of wisdom, to their lawful use. It inspires, develops, cultivates, and matures all the fine-toned sympathies, joys, tastes, kindred feelings, and affections of our nature. It inspires virtue, kindness, goodness, tenderness, gentleness, and charity. It develops beauty of person, form, and features. It tends to health, vigor, animation, and social feeling. It invigorates all the faculties of the physical and intellectual man. It strengthens and gives tone to the nerves. In short, it is, as it were, marrow to the bone, joy to the heart, light to the eyes, music to the ears, and life to the whole being. (Parley P. Pratt, *Key to the Science of Theology,* Deseret Book Company, 1978, page 61.)

"The gospel makes evil minded men good, and good men better and women and children better than they have ever been before." (Hartman Rector, Jr., "A Gospel of Conversion," *Ensign,* January 1981, page 4.) Let it do that for you. It is not some remote religious philosophy. It is life. It is current. It can help you live in today's world.

A stake president in Canada counseled the members in his stake to study the conference talks of President Kimball. Then, for the next six months, he instructed them to apply the words of the prophet to their lives, just as they did the standard works. He reasoned this way, "The Lord did not give the instructions for the ark to Adam, he did not give the instructions for moving the children of Israel out of Egypt to Noah; he gave the instructions for the times to the prophet of that time. There is no reason to believe that things are any different now. If we are to prepare for whatever is coming, we must listen to the Lord's mouthpiece of this time."

I think that is exciting. This is truly a gospel that can help us to return to our Father's presence. We must heed the counsel, accept the gift of the Atonement, and do everything we can to incorporate the fulness of the gospel into our individual homes. Study the scriptures and the messages of the Brethren; pray earnestly and specifically morning and night; give service cheerfully; teach your children; keep the commandments; be repentant; pay your tithes and offerings willingly; keep the Word of Wisdom; get prepared individually and as a family; and seek for excellence in your life.

List every word or phrase or activity that comes to your mind as you concentrate on what living the gospel means to you. Your list probably is long. Do you feel overwhelmed by it—does it seem more than you can handle? Well, live the basic principles and all else that you possibly can according to the season or time of life you are in. The Lord looks at the intent of your heart. He doesn't want you to feel discouraged and weighted down. He wants you to keep the commandments and do all you can. You can't do everything all at once, but you can do all you are able. He will know whether you are making the effort.

I feel that I can't leave this topic without saying something about the Sabbath. Keeping it holy is often fraught with negative connotations. Try to draw up a list of things you *can* do on the Sabbath which would serve to bring you closer to the Lord and to your family. You can study the gospel, hold family council, write in your journal, write to loved ones, visit or have people in, do genealogy, listen to uplifting music, play an instrument or sing suitable songs, tell children stories of the history of the Church, view slide presentations borrowed from the meetinghouse library, play quiet Sunday games together.

Your home can be a holy place. Let the gospel permeate every area of your life. Let it add depth and beauty to your life as you strive to dedicate yourself to living in such a way that you will become perfected, along with the Saints of God.

May your home be filled with the Spirit and may you and your family always seek "first the kingdom of God, and his righteousness; and all these things shall be added unto you" (Matthew 6:33).

14

Being Your Best Self

All through this book I have tried to get you to look at things from your own perspective, to find out how you feel about things, to discover what you think, and, in short, to find out what kind of person you are.

You see, throughout your childhood years, you were busy trying to please mom and dad because you felt good when you did that. They smiled at you and told you they loved you.

Then you spent another span of years as a teenager questioning just about everything you had so cheerfully accepted in childhood.

I see this as a time when you threw up your personality, values, beliefs, likes, and dislikes into the air, then, as they all came down, you tried to fit all the pieces together into an acceptable pattern.

Well, most of you are not too far removed from that stage, and now you must define your new role as wife and mother, which can be pretty hard.

If you don't see a definite pattern forming, relax. Not many girls know exactly what kind of person they are becoming.

Even a partial identification at this stage of your life can certainly cut down on your frustrations and help to increase your enjoyment. For example, maybe you've always wished you were 5' 10" and a strong swimmer and basketball star like your older sister; but in fact you are 5' 1", musical, delicate, and lacking the physical stamina your sister has.

Is there any way you can change your height? Do you think that sports are really more valid than music? Do you feel you are inferior to your sister?

Would it help you to know that over in another house there is a 5' 10" woman who loves biology so she became a marine biologist. She enjoys her work, but secretly she wishes she were tiny and musical like you. She feels that she is not as much a woman as little feminine you.

This is one of the greatest wastes in humanity — this reluctance to accept your own gifts, abilities, aptitudes, and inclinations as being just as valid as anyone else's. Why do some girls always have to wish they were someone other than what they are? It is the extreme case of thinking the grass is greener in the next yard.

Did you ever stop to think that perhaps the reason that grass over there seems so much better than your own is because you don't know how much crab grass is mixed in with it or where the holes are?

Insecurity, the fear that what you are is not as good as what someone else is, is very prevalent among young women. The LDS woman is further concerned because she fears that everyone is perfect except her. Nonsense!

I want to urge you one final time — accept yourself, make what improvements you wish, strive for excellence, and work toward the ultimate goal of becoming a celestial wife, a perfected being, but of your own kind.

So often you wish you were like someone else. If you could see what her life is really like beneath the facade she shows you, perhaps you would find that her conflicts and problems are far more troublesome than your own. Do not waste any more time wishing you were someone else.

Do not compare yourself to others. Instead, compare the *you* of today with the *you* of five years ago. Have you made any progress? Now, what about the *you* ten years down the road? That is the relevant question: Who am I now and who do I want to become?

Maybe a good place to start is by noting all the things that you are *not*. I was past forty when I finally had the courage and confidence to face what I was not and never would be. I knew I was not an athlete. Why it took so long to come to this conclusion when the evidence was so overwhelming, I do not know. I don't even like sports, but my husband is an athlete and all the children are quite skilled that way. I felt inferior. Further, I finally accepted that, a degree in home economics notwithstanding, home arts were not my strongest interest. That was hard to accept, especially in an LDS environment. And, peaceful and serene I would never be, not totally. Then, one last hurdle was recognizing that although my mother was a tiny 5' 0", I could never be that. That may seem trivial to you, but for the first half of my life I felt that, because I was not those things, I was somehow inferior. Do any of those thoughts sound familiar?

The day I was finally able to look at myself and see what kind of woman I was, was the day I really started to relax and quit worrying about myself. I became more concerned about others. It was the best thing that ever could have happened. Certainly, there are many goals I am trying to achieve, and there are many improvements I am working on, but my basic self is no longer under fire. I am building on that self. Do you see the difference?

It's rather like wanting to make a dress. You know what kind of material you have bought, but you don't feel it is as pretty as Louise's, or Julie's, or Janae's. So, instead of setting to work choosing the pattern, cutting it out, getting it sewn and enjoying it, you keep fretting. As long as you keep thinking your piece is no good because it is not like someone else's, you make no progress on building your own dress.

But, once you finally come to grips with it, and you are able to accept your piece although it is not like the others, you are ready to start to create the best garment you can from that piece of fabric.

I hate to think of you wandering around for forty years not knowing whether or not you like who you are. I hope that there may be some ideas here that will help you to make your discovery sooner and thereby increase your productivity and happiness.

Every one of you has been endowed with many talents and gifts. "Neglect not the gift that is in thee, which was given thee by prophecy" (1 Timothy 4:14), and "to every man is given a gift by the Spirit of God" (D&C 46:11).

To underline how very important this is to our mortal lives, I quote Elder Sterling W. Sill:

> If there is one thing of which I am completely certain in my own mind, it is that the one business of life is to succeed. I am absolutely certain that God did not create this beautiful earth for our benefit with all of its laws, resources, and opportunities, without having something very important in mind for those who would live upon it. It would be completely unreasonable for God to create us in his own image, give us his own personal form, endow us with these potentially magnificent minds, these miraculous personalities, and these fantastic physical powers, and then expect us to waste our lives in failure. And yet I am sure of this, that the greatest waste in the world is that you and I live so far below the level of our possibilities." ("The One Business of Life," *Ensign,* January 1981, page 51.)

Were you aware that you are living below the level of your possibilities? Do you have any idea what your possibilities are? Be assured that you are much more capable than you ever give yourself credit for being.

Do not put yourself down. You may keep telling yourself and anyone who will listen that you are just an ordinary girl with no talents or gifts. As long as you believe that, you will keep proving that it is true. Your thinking will limit you. You cannot be what you do not believe you can be. You are the one who makes the choice.

I want to challenge you to discover what kind of basic fabric you are, then to strive for excellence as you develop that fabric of yourself. "All things are possible to him that believeth." (Mark 9:23.)

The power of positive thinking is not some wonder that the psychologists have discovered, it is truth that the Lord outlined many centuries ago. The first step in becoming a better, happier, more effective person is based on your own attitude—you must believe in yourself. Believe that you truly are a daughter of God, believe that you have the potential to be exalted, to live in the celestial kingdom with your husband and children. Believe that you can live a happy and productive life here in mortality.

Do not be satisfied with less than what you know you can be. Do not be contented with mediocrity. Do not accept a nonproductive and boring life.

Promise yourself and the Lord that you will put forth real effort to do the best job of whatever you are doing and to become the best that you are capable of becoming. Go ahead, enlarge your scope. Enlarge your soul.

No matter what your particular inclinations, talents, or aptitudes, recognize that by developing them you can become an interesting, effective, and vital person.

Perhaps you have never stopped to consider the tremendous instrument you carry around under your skull. You have potential which no man has ever been able to adequately measure.

Your mind is composed of over ten billion tiny cells called neurons. In a computer, each of these neurons would be represented by a tiny transistor. The cost of these transistors alone would be well over $1 billion (1976-77 prices) but this would just be the beginning, for each of these units would have to be connected. The interconnecting nerve fibers at the brain stagger the imagination.

If you could take all of the communication systems of the world and compress them into the size of your brain, they would still represent only a small part of the infinite lengths of nerve fibers that connect the transistor cells of your mind. If such an assembly could be achieved, the resulting machine would cost over three billion, billion dollars (1976-77 prices), occupy an area about the size of an airplane hangar, be over twenty stories tall, and require the power of Niagara Falls to keep it going.

Even then, it could only do a fraction of what your mind can do, for it could not know itself, create, have a self will, think thoughts of its choice, or have feeling.

Considering your brain, then, weighs only three pounds, and is about the size of a half a grapefruit, you can begin to comprehend the marvel of this gift of yours: the mind. (Adventures in Attitudes, cassette tape, Personal Dynamics Institute, Minneapolis, 1967.)

I guess I could go on and on, but there is no need for it. I hope you've caught some slight vision of what life on earth can be for you. It is up to you to decide if it will be boring and miserable, or challenging, rewarding and exciting.

You have within you a mind, a heart, and a spirit, plus the ability to control how you will perceive this existence. You can pick up on the talents and abilities and interests you find inside yourself. You can develop these so that your days, and the days of your family, are filled with discovery, accomplishment and enjoyment.

Sure, you are going to be busy looking after babies for several years, but that doesn't mean your mind has to go into neutral. You must take some time each day to fill yourself so you will have something to give to your husband and your little children.

Women are givers, as Anne Morrow Lindbergh said, but eventually their "spring is dry; the well is empty." (*Gift from the Sea,* page 48.) A woman must take whatever steps necessary to replenish herself so she will have something to give to those who depend on her. It is good advice, and is the thing which kept me relatively sane during the very hectic years when our big three were all preschoolers. Our Jean-Ann was three and Karen was sixteen months when Calvin was born. Two weeks before Calvin's sixth birthday, Earl was born. I credit Anne Morrow Lindbergh's concept of the importance for a woman to have some time to herself for keeping me in the land of the productive and happy people.

Do not feel guilty. Look on it as preventive medicine.

You'll recall that the Lord said to "love thy neighbor as thyself" (Matthew 19:19). He did not say love thy neighbor instead of thyself. The Lord is wise. He knows you cannot feel love for others while you are starved for acceptance and self-esteem.

So, take a little time for yourself to do something you enjoy, to learn something, to develop a skill so you will be able to truly love others. This life is a glorious life, a preparation for exaltation. Do not shortchange yourself. Make the most of every day.

I have loved writing this book. For over a year I have worked at it more or less nonstop, and never once did I lose interest in it. There have been days when it dragged, when I have felt a stupor of thought and have had to rewrite. Even then, I never did want to quit.

There have been other days when I have felt uplifted and unable to keep up with thoughts as they poured forth. These were the days I thanked the Lord for giving me the desire to do this. And now that it's finished I feel exhilarated and also a little sad.

I want all of you and my own two daughters and the two girls who will someday marry my sons to experience life deeply, with a sense of wonder and appreciation.

The Lord does live, Jesus is the Christ, we do have prophets in this day, and it definitely is possible to return to the exalted presence of our Heavenly Father. I know this to be true.

I want to close with this story and hope that as you read it, you will know that your ticket on this earth entitles you to all the choice experiences, the best and sweetest that this life has to offer.

There was once a humble little lady who had spent her whole life cleaning other people's houses. Each day she would work for ten to twelve hours polishing, vacuuming, and scrubbing some of the most elegant homes in her city.

Then she would return to her little single room basement suite and count her meager earnings. More than anything, she wanted to take an ocean cruise. She didn't want to cruise along the west coast of the United States and Canada—she wanted to cruise on the blue Mediterranean Sea. That was her one dream.

Well, you must realize that her earnings as a cleaning woman did not amount to a great deal, and after she had paid her rent, utilities, food, and other necessities, her savings were pitifully small.

Inflation continued to rise, and she just never seemed to be able to quite scrape together enough to pay for the flight to Europe plus the cost of the cruise. She kept looking at the travel brochures, saving and dreaming.

Years and years passed by and her desire to go did never diminish. It was the single driving force of her life.

Finally, she saved just enough money, and she was happy because soon she would be too old to work. The last month of work she carefully packed her things as well as a basket of dried fruit, crackers, cheese, and whatever she could afford that would not perish.

She clutched her tickets in her work-worn hands and took off for the adventure she had worked a whole lifetime to achieve. Everything was marvelous. The Mediterranean was a deeper blue and more beautiful than she had imagined. She felt as though she had gone to paradise.

She sat up on deck most of the day, but as soon as the meal bells would ring she would silently slip down to her cabin and eat from her hoard of supplies.

Finally, it was the last night out, and just before the dinner bell rang the ship's captain sought her out where she sat enjoying the evening sun.

He took her hand and said, "I make a practice during each cruise to have everyone on board sit at least once with me at the captain's table for one meal. You are one of the few people who has not yet joined me. The steward tells me you never eat in the dining room. Is anything wrong? I would like to invite you to sit with me tonight."

Embarrassed, the little lady mumbled, "Oh, captain, I can't afford to eat with all you grand people in the dining room. But, I don't mind. You see, I wanted to go on this cruise so badly, I really didn't mind having to bring my own food."

The captain held her gnarled hands in his, and for a moment he could neither look at her nor speak. He seemed to understand what she had endured for these two weeks in the sun.

Then, very quietly and gently he said, "Madam, when you paid for your cruise ticket, you also paid for all your meals in the ship's dining room. Your ticket entitled you to anything or everything on the menu. Please — come this last night and dine with me at my table."

For the five special
people in my life:

Hank
Jean-Ann
Karen
Calvin
Earl

Library of Congress Catalog Card Number: 81-69199
ISBN 0-88494-435-2

First Printing, 1981

Lithographed in the United States of America
PUBLISHERS PRESS
Salt Lake City, Utah

H A P P I L Y
E V E R
A F T E R ?

Putting Vitality and Reality into Marriage

Jeannie Takahashi

BOOKCRAFT·SALT LAKE CITY, UTAH